Daniel

The Man Who Walked
Against the World

Table of Contents

Chapter 1 – Counter-Cultural Faith: The Call to Walk Against the World 10

    1.0 Opening Orientation—What Is "Walking Against the World"? 11

    1.1 The Biblical Mandate for Holiness 12

    1.2 Cultural Pressures Then and Now 14

    1.3 Why Standing Alone Matters 17

    1.4 Mapping Daniel's Book for the Journey Ahead 20

    1.5 Method and Framework for This Book 23

    1.6 Spiritual Disciplines That Sustain Resistance.................26

Chapter 2 – Exile and Identity: Daniel's Early Tests 31

    2.0 Setting the Stage—From Jerusalem's Ashes to Babylon's Gates 31

    2.1 The Trauma of Deportation 33

    2.2 Renaming and Re-education..35

    2.3 The Food Test—Table Fellowship as Theological Boundary 38

    2.4 Identity Formation in Exile: Practices and Postures 41

    2.5 Contemporary Parallels—Exile at the Office, Campus, and Online 44

    2.6 Spiritual Habits That Anchor Identity 46

Chapter 3 – The Discipline of Devotion: Prayer and Wisdom under Pressure 50

    3.0 Situating Devotion in an Age of Anxious Empires..........50

3.1 The Crisis of the Forgotten Dream (Daniel 2) 51

3.2 A Theology of Prayerful Dependence 55

3.3 Practising Devotion in High-Performance Cultures 58

3.4 Discernment and Revelation—Translating Insight into Action 62

3.5 Cultivating Communities of Disciplined Devotion 64

3.6 Devotion Turned Public Service 66

Chapter 4 – Serving with Integrity: Daniel the Statesman and Interpreter 70

4.0 From Exile to Cabinet—Spiritual Foundations for Public Service 70

4.1 Promotion to Chief of the Wise Men 74

4.2 Interpreting Dreams and Shaping Policy 78

4.3 Integrity under Scrutiny—Political Jealousy and Court Intrigue 81

4.4 Integrating Faith and Vocation Today 85

4.5 Contemporary Case Studies—Modern "Daniels" in Government, Business, and NGOs 87

4.6 The Liturgy of Leadership—Practices that Sustain Integrity 89

4.7 Fiery Faith in the Furnace of Public Opinion 92

Chapter 5 – Fiery Faith: Hananiah, Mishael, and Azariah in the Furnace 96

5.0 Crucible of Conscience—Setting the Stage for Defiant Worship 96

5.1 The Image of Gold and Imperial Idolatry 99

5.2 Civil Disobedience and Non-violent Resistance 101

5.3 Solidarity in Suffering—Strength in Shared Conviction

.... 103

5.4 Modern Idols and the Cost of Loyalty 105

5.5 Practising Fiery Faith Today—Disciplines of Defiant Worship 109

5.6 Writing on the Wall: Calling a Culture to Account 111

Chapter 6 – Warning a Decadent Culture: Belshazzar and the Writing on the Wall 115

6.0 Banquet on the Brink—Framing the Fall of an Empire .115

6.1 The Last Night of Babylon (539 BC) 118

6.2 Mene, Tekel, Parsin—The Divine Audit 120

6.3 Diagnostic Lessons for Contemporary Societies 122

6.4 Forming Prophetic Communities—Practices for Cultural Discernment... 126

6.5 Faithfulness in the Lion's Den 129

Chapter 7 – Faithfulness in the Lion's Den: Perseverance amid Systemic Opposition... 131

7.0 Behind Palace Walls—Why Integrity Provokes Bureaucratic Backlash 131

7.1 Political Manipulation and Prayer Bans 132

7.2 Deliverance and Vindication 135

7.3 Persevering under Institutional Hostility Today 137

7.4 Disciplines that Fortify Lions'-Den Faith 140

7.5 Apocalyptic Vision and Hope beyond Empires 142

Chapter 8 – Vision of the Ages: Apocalyptic Hope and Eschatological Courage 145

8.0 Reading Apocalyptic—Why Symbolic Visions Matter for Everyday Saints 145

- 8.1 The Four Beasts and the Ancient of Days (Daniel 7) 148
- 8.2 Ram, Goat, and the Little Horn (Daniel 8) 150
- 8.3 Seventy Weeks Prophecy (Daniel 9) 152
- 8.4 Final Conflict and Resurrection (Daniel 10–12) 154
- 8.5 How Apocalyptic Vision Shapes Present Conduct 156
- 8.6 Pilgrims of Hope in a Fragmented World 158

Chapter 9 – Walking Against the World Today: Contemporary Issues and Biblical Wisdom 161

- 9.0 Exiles in Every Epoch—Why Daniel's Model Still Speaks 161
- 9.1 Secularism and Moral Relativism 162
- 9.2 Sexual Ethics and Gender Ideology 165
- 9.3 Technology, Surveillance, and Conformity 167
- 9.4 Economic Pressures and Integrity 170
- 9.5 Political Polarization and Kingdom Allegiance 172
- 9.6 Crafting a Contemporary Rule of Resistance 174
- 9.7 Bridge to the Epilogue—Heirs of an Unshakable Kingdom 176

Chapter 10 – Living Daniel's Legacy: Forming Counter-Cultural Communities 179

- 10.0 Why Communities Matter—From Lone Exiles to Prophetic Households 180
- 10.1 Spiritual Disciplines for Resistance 181
- 10.2 Mentorship and Inter-Generational Transmission 183
- 10.3 Missional Presence in the Public Square 184
- 10.4 Crafting a Rule of Life 187
- 10.5 Living in Maranatha Expectancy—Hope that Outlasts

Empires..189

10.5 Living in Maranatha Expectancy—Hope that Outlasts
Empires..190

10.6 Bridge to the Closing Benediction—From Ancient
Courts to Modern Cities 191

Chapter 1 – Counter-Cultural Faith: The Call to Walk Against the World

From the dusty plains of Judah to the glittering courts of Babylon, the life of Daniel unfolds as a vivid portrait of unwavering allegiance in the face of overwhelming pressure. In an age when cultural currents swirl around us—demanding our attention, our trust, even our very identity—Daniel's story speaks across the centuries with remarkable clarity. He did not retreat into a hermitage; nor did he cloak his convictions in vague generalities. Instead, he embraced public service, rigorous devotion, and prophetic boldness, demonstrating that genuine faith neither hides from the world nor capitulates to its demands. His example shows that true holiness is not an abstract ideal but a lived reality that engages families, workplaces, and civic structures with integrity.

Walking against prevailing winds requires more than moral exhortation; it calls for a transformation of heart, mind, and community. As we embark on this chapter, we will undergird our journey with the conviction that God's kingdom reshapes every sphere of human life. The posture Daniel modeled—kneeling in prayer, standing firm in peril, interpreting dreams with humility—offers a rhythm for believers today. It invites us to realign our schedules, our loyalties, and our imaginations with the purposes of the Ancient of Days. Whether one confronts subtle demands for compromise in boardrooms or overt coercion in public policy debates, the same unwavering trust that upheld Daniel can anchor us.

This chapter lays the groundwork for a counter-cultural pilgrimage, inviting readers to discover how divine sovereignty, personal character, and communal witness interweave to form a robust faith. We begin by tracing the scriptural call to distinctiveness that pulses through both Testaments, then shine a light on the trenchant pressures that have always sought to absorb God's people. We explore why isolated obedience can catalyze widespread renewal, and we map the very structure of Daniel's testimony—from palace intrigues to apocalyptic visions—to guide our own sense-making. Finally, we introduce the spiritual disciplines that fortify resistance, ensuring that our convictions survive both daylight scrutiny and midnight trials.

As we set foot on this path, may the same Spirit who empowered Daniel kindle within us a confidence unshaken by shifting sands of culture. May our eyes fix on the One whose kingdom never falters, and may our lives become living letters that announce His reign to every generation.

1.0 Opening Orientation—What Is "Walking Against the World"?

The phrase "walking against the world" may sound confrontational, yet Scripture consistently portrays godly resistance as a life-giving pilgrimage rather than a hostile standoff. The biblical writers use the term **kosmos** in at least two ways: first to celebrate the created order God declared "very good" in Genesis 1, and second to describe the fallen cultural system that sets itself in opposition to the Creator (1 John 2:15-17). Recognizing these two meanings keeps believers from confusing hostility toward sin with disdain for creation itself. In the Garden, Adam and Eve were called to cultivate the earth in fellowship with God, but after the fall, humanity organized itself around power, violence, and pride, culminating in Babel's agenda to secure self-glorification apart from heaven (Genesis 11:1-9). The prophets later coined the term "Babylon" to symbolize every empire that exalts itself above the knowledge of God, a motif that culminates in Revelation 18. Jesus echoes the same polarity when He tells His disciples they are "in the world" yet "not of it" (John 17:14-18). The tension confronts Christians today: how to participate in culture for the common good without being pressed into its idolatrous mold. That tension frames the journey this chapter inaugurates. By examining Daniel's life, readers will see that resistance is less about withdrawal and more about worship that exposes counterfeit gods. The discipline of discerning which cultural liturgies form us is indispensable for faithfulness, whether those liturgies involve ancient feasts in Nebuchadnezzar's palace or the steady scroll of twenty-first-century social media. Seeing resistance as an act of love for God and neighbor guards us from smug separatism. Daniel did not despise the Babylonians he served; he prayed for them, interpreted their dreams, and saved their sages from unjust execution. The same Spirit calls believers to engage their neighbors with humility grounded in holiness. Only by grasping this big-picture framework can we navigate the details of diet choices, prayer habits, and ethical convictions that follow. This orientation therefore prepares us to explore the biblical mandate for holiness, which forms the bedrock of counter-cultural living.

1.1 The Biblical Mandate for Holiness

1.1.1 Set-Apart Identity in the Pentateuch

Holiness in the Pentateuch is not cosmetic purification but covenant allegiance that reshapes every sphere of life. Leviticus employs the root **qādôš** more than any other book, anchoring Israel's call to mirror Yahweh's character: "Be holy, for I am holy" (Leviticus 11:44-45). Circumcision embodied a total consecration of future generations to God's promise (Genesis 17:9-14). Dietary boundaries underscored dependence on divine provision and reminded Israel daily that even mundane appetites must bow to covenant lordship. Sabbath rhythms rewrote economic and social expectations by declaring that productivity never outranks worship (Exodus 20:8-11). The feast calendar trained the nation's memory to revolve around redemption events like Passover, foreshadowing Christ's atoning work (1 Corinthians 5:7). Israel's camp layout placed the tabernacle at its center, visually preaching that God's presence defines national identity. Even clothing mixtures and field margins hinted that boundaries matter in a world prone to confusion and greed. Yet these outward markers aimed beyond mere difference; they invited surrounding nations to ponder a kingdom of justice and mercy (Deuteronomy 4:6-8). When Israel embraced holiness, strangers and sojourners found refuge under Torah's protection (Leviticus 19:33-34). Tragically, idolatry often eclipsed mission, revealing that external symbols cannot substitute for a circumcised heart (Deuteronomy 10:16). Daniel's story will revisit these Pentateuchal themes, showing how an exile can embody holiness without access to temple sacrifices. The foundational logic of consecration therefore leads naturally to the prophetic era, where the call to distinctiveness takes on new urgency amid impending judgment.

1.1.2 Prophetic Calls to Distinctiveness

Isaiah envisions a remnant purified by fire who will bear the title "holy seed" (Isaiah 6:13), suggesting that holiness is both a refining and reproductive force. He invites Zion to depart from Babylon's defilement while carrying the vessels of the Lord with reverence (Isaiah 52:11), a charge that Daniel himself would later model by refusing to partake of the king's wine. Jeremiah, writing to exiles in the very city Daniel served, urges them to seek Babylon's welfare without yielding to its idols (Jeremiah 29:4-7), blending civic engagement with covenant fidelity. Ezekiel dramatizes the cost of compromise through sign-acts, lying on his side and shaving his hair to warn that diluted holiness breeds devastating exile (Ezekiel 5:1-4). The minor prophets amplify the same dual note of indictment and invitation: Hosea's marital pain exposes Israel's adulterous alliances, while Micah contrasts corrupt Jerusalem elites with a coming shepherd-king who will rule in the Lord's strength (Micah 5:2-4). Each prophetic oracle reminds the community that holiness is communal and ethical, not merely ritual. Justice toward the poor, honesty in commerce, and purity in worship are woven together in God's tapestry of distinctiveness. The exile thus becomes both punishment and purification, pruning the nation for future fruitfulness. Daniel's narrative lands precisely at this prophetic inflection point, illustrating how individuals within a compromised culture may still live out the prophets' vision. His obedience demonstrates that prophetic holiness is not antiquated idealism but practical wisdom for hostile environments. This trajectory from Sinai to the prophets seamlessly opens the door to the fullness of holiness revealed in Christ and the apostolic witness.

1.1.3 Christ and Apostolic Non-Conformity

Jesus consummates Israel's call by embodied holiness that welcomes sinners while never endorsing sin. His Sermon on the Mount redefines righteousness from external compliance to internal transformation, declaring the meek, the merciful, and the pure in heart blessed in a world that prizes power (Matthew 5:3-12). He contrasts two gates and two roads, advising disciples to choose the narrow way that leads to life, not the broad path of cultural accommodation (Matthew 7:13-14). He models table fellowship that bridges social divides yet refuses exploitation, overturning merchants' tables in the temple to defend God's honor (John 2:13-17). Paul builds on this ethos, beseeching believers to present their bodies as living sacrifices and to resist being conformed to the age, instead being transformed by renewed minds (Romans 12:1-2). He labels the church a "new creation" (2 Corinthians 5:17), signaling a break with the old order. Peter characterizes believers as exiles and sojourners whose citizenship lies elsewhere, calling them to holiness rooted in the Lamb's precious blood (1 Peter 1:14-19; 2:11). Hebrews exhorts the community to "go to Him outside the camp, bearing His reproach," indicating that allegiance to Jesus may cost social acceptance (Hebrews 13:12-14). John warns that friendship with the world system is incompatible with love for the Father (1 John 2:15), framing discipleship as a decisive transfer of loyalties. Collectively, these apostolic voices reinforce that holiness is Christocentric, Spirit-empowered, and missional. They supply the theological oxygen Daniel's example breathes, offering Christians today a robust framework for resistance that is neither legalistic nor escapist. With the mandate thus traced from Pentateuch to apostles, the discussion can now address concrete cultural pressures that threaten to erode distinctiveness in every generation.

1.2 Cultural Pressures Then and Now

1.2.1 Babylon's Ideological Program (6th c. BC)

Nebuchadnezzar's imperial strategy targeted identity at its roots, beginning with the forced deportation of Jerusalem's elite youth in 605 BC (Daniel 1:3-4). Select captives were renamed to sever covenantal connections—Daniel ("God is my judge") became

Belteshazzar ("May Bel protect the king"), a verbal attempt to rewrite spiritual allegiance. The three-year curriculum in the language and literature of the Chaldeans offered more than academic enrichment; it immersed students in astrology, omens, and myths that deified the Babylonian state. Daily rations from the king's table symbolized dependence on imperial favor, an early form of soft power designed to nurture gratitude and compliance. The king's dream statute in chapter 2 revealed the empire's self-perception as the golden head of successive world kingdoms, tempting subjects to bow to inevitable "progress." Shadrach, Meshach, and Abednego's furnace ordeal exposed how totalitarian regimes fuse political loyalty with religious worship, punishing dissent as treason. Public spectacle played a critical role: the fiery furnace was located on the Dura plain, ensuring that resistance—or submission—became communal theater. State propaganda was reinforced by socioeconomic incentives, promising advancement to compliant sages and extermination for dissenters. Even successful interpreters like Daniel had to steward influence cautiously, lest proximity to power dilute prophetic clarity. The empire's racial and religious pluralism masked a coercive core that demanded ultimate homage to Babylon's gods. Daniel's quiet refusal of royal food demonstrated that holiness begins with hidden choices long before it becomes visible heroism. His subsequent rise in administration illustrates God's ability to honor fidelity without endorsing the empire's ideology. By tracing these historical pressures, readers gain a template for spotting analogous mechanisms in modern societies, bridging naturally to an exploration of contemporary formation engines.

1.2.2 Formation Mechanisms in Late-Modern Culture

While twenty-first-century Western democracies lack a single monarch, they wield equally potent tools of identity formation through ubiquitous technology and consumer marketing. Global streaming platforms curate narratives that normalize relativistic ethics and present self-actualization as life's supreme goal. Social media algorithms learn users' desires and reinforce them, functioning as invisible tutors that disciple emotions toward envy or outrage. The advertising industry infiltrates daily routines, persuading viewers that happiness is only one purchase away, echoing Babylon's banquet by offering indulgence as belonging.

University environments often frame faith as at best a private preference, at worst an oppressive relic, subtly pressuring students to compartmentalize spirituality. Corporate cultures prize productivity, making Sabbath rest feel irresponsible and thereby eroding a primary biblical marker of trust. Sexual ethics have shifted from covenant commitment to consent-based autonomy, labeling chastity as repressive nostalgia. Digital pornography provides a low-commitment simulation of intimacy, undermining the covenantal imagination central to biblical holiness. Political discourse increasingly operates in echo chambers, disciplining participants to demonize opponents rather than pursue neighbor love. Even churches risk adopting consumer logic by branding worship as a spiritual product to be consumed rather than a sacrifice of praise (Hebrews 13:15). Data surveillance economies trade convenience for privacy, normalizing constant observation reminiscent of the ever-watchful eye of Babylon's bureaucrats. In this milieu, believers face the temptation to curate an online persona that garners approval at the cost of integrity. Yet these pressures also offer opportunities: public platforms can amplify counter-cultural testimonies, and work environments may honor excellence that springs from God-given wisdom. Understanding these mechanisms sets the stage for comparing ancient and modern empires, highlighting transferable insights without collapsing their distinct contexts.

1.2.3 Comparative Analysis: Ancient Empire & Digital Babylon

Both Nebuchadnezzar's Babylon and the digital age impose formative liturgies that shape loves, loyalties, and imaginations. Babylon leveraged visible statues and decrees, whereas digital algorithms employ personalization, making conformity appear self-generated. Yet each system promises security—military might then, technological convenience now—in exchange for unquestioned allegiance. Renaming in the exile parallels modern identity construction through avatars and usernames that can obscure God-given vocations. The communal pressure of the Dura plain finds its analogy in viral trends that punish dissent through social shaming or cancellation. However, contemporary pluralism allows for localized micro-cultures, which can either cushion faith communities or isolate believers in echo chambers lacking prophetic cross-pollination. Ancient Babylon enforced religious uniformity under threat of death; modern societies often enforce ideological conformity through economic marginalization and reputational damage rather than physical harm. Both contexts reveal the subtle danger of incremental compromise: Daniel's diet test mirrors daily choices about entertainment, spending, and speech that seem trivial yet train allegiance over time. Ancient empires operated on lunar calendars and astrological omens, while the digital empire quantifies everything with data, but each offers counterfeit means of securing the future apart from divine revelation. Recognizing these parallels equips Christians to adopt Daniel-like strategies: intentional community, disciplined prayer rhythms, vocational excellence, and respectful non-compliance when conscience demands. This analytic synthesis transitions the discussion toward the motivations for standing alone, which will unpack why resistance is worth the cost and how it shapes both witness and character in the chapters that follow.

1.3 Why Standing Alone Matters

1.3.1 Public Witness to God's Sovereignty

When a single life refuses to bow before prevailing idols, it functions as a living placard announcing that another throne governs history. Daniel's earliest act of gentle defiance—requesting vegetables and water instead of royal delicacies—seemed inconsequential, yet it culminated in Nebuchadnezzar's open confession that "your God is God of gods and Lord of kings" (Daniel 2:47). Small obediences, publicly observed, create fissures in the cultural narrative that power or popularity is ultimate. Jesus frames this logic when He calls disciples a city on a hill whose good works cause onlookers to glorify the Father (Matthew 5:14–16). Such witness is never mere propaganda; it is enacted theology, demonstrating that God alone sustains His servants. Public fidelity also corrects distorted images of holiness that equate piety with withdrawal; Daniel served faithfully within pagan structures while reserving ultimate allegiance for Yahweh, showing that faith need not evacuate the public square. Modern parallels abound when executives refuse fraudulent accounting despite pressure from shareholders, or when students decline cheating even at the risk of scholarships, thereby naming God as higher authority without pronouncing a single sermon. The very visibility of integrity invites questions, positioning the believer as steward of a story larger than personal preference (1 Peter 3:15). Corporate boardrooms, political forums, and neighborhood associations may never host formal altar calls, but they become arenas where consistent righteousness unveils divine kingship. When believers remain calm amid crisis, they incarnate the conviction that circumstances, however dire, are bounded by goodness sovereignly orchestrated (Romans 8:28). Such calmness is not stoic detachment but trust rooted in God's unassailable throne, a theme Daniel repeatedly emphasizes in his speeches before monarchs. Today's public witness is amplified through digital footprints; integrity displayed on social platforms travels farther than ancient edicts, magnifying either righteousness or compromise. Wise stewardship of that reach means curating authenticity, not performance, so that God's glory rather than personal branding stays central. Even silent actions—like stepping away from gossip threads—speak loudly because they interrupt default patterns and force reconsideration of assumed norms. Every workplace memo, classroom debate, or neighborhood initiative thus offers potential stage time for God's sovereignty to be dramatized. The Spirit leverages such moments to awaken curiosity in observers who once dismissed faith as private sentimentality. Daniel's example affirms the principle that visible allegiance, though risky, catalyzes revelation about the One who "changes times and seasons, removes kings and sets up kings" (Daniel 2:21). This outward testimony naturally raises the question of inward resilience, for public courage must be forged in the crucible of character before it can withstand scrutiny.

1.3.2 Character Formation Through Testing

Tests are God's chosen gymnasium where souls develop the muscle memory of holiness. James insists that trials, when received with trust, mature believers into complete people lacking nothing (James 1:2–4). Daniel's long apprenticeship in Babylon—spanning dietary restrictions, death-threat dreams, and lion-infested legislation—created layer upon layer of habitual dependence on God. Each episode escalated the stakes, forging perseverance the way repeated hammer strikes strengthen tempered steel. Modern neuroscience corroborates this pattern, noting that habits of integrity carve neural pathways that make future obedience more reflexive. Yet biblical formation surpasses mere behavioral conditioning; it is Spirit-empowered transformation that shapes affections, reorders loves, and re-imprints identity as children of the Holy One (Romans 5:3–5). Tests surface hidden loyalties, revealing whether security rests in divine faithfulness or social applause. Daniel's willingness to lose both position and life if necessary exposed the fragile ephemerality of Babylonian accolades. Contemporary believers face subtler crucibles—perhaps a promotion contingent on ethical compromise, or academic acclaim contingent on denying moral absolutes. In each scenario, repeated choice crafts either a holy reflex or a pattern of capitulation. Scripture attests that endurance is not self-generated grit but fruit of faith that fixes eyes on the unseen (Hebrews 12:1–2). Daniel undoubtedly rehearsed God's past deliverances, allowing memory to supply courage for fresh threats. Modern disciples can imitate this by cataloguing answered prayers and meditating on biographies of saints who endured, allowing testimony to tutor temperament. Testing also weaves humility into strength; deliverance from lions credited to angelic intervention kept Daniel from self-congratulation, just as Paul's thorn maintained reliance on grace (2 Corinthians 12:9). When suffering accompanies fidelity, character gains the gravitas to empathize with others' weaknesses, transforming isolated heroes into compassionate shepherds. Such seasoned character becomes the seedbed for communal influence, because people instinctively trust leaders whose convictions have been stress-tested. Thus the forge of testing prepares the steel that will support others in their hour of trial, leading naturally to the ripple effects that radiate from one steadfast life.

1.3.3 Ripple Effects: Inspiring Communities of Resistance

Courage tends to be contagious, and Daniel's steadfastness ignited courage in peers and rulers alike. His three friends found faith to withstand the furnace in part because they had watched Daniel risk his status over food in chapter 1—an illustration that individual obedience seeds collective boldness. Sociologists observe that moral shifts often reach tipping points when a critical minority normalizes dissent, demonstrating the power of catalytic examples. Scripture describes this dynamic through metaphors of leaven and mustard seeds, small yet influential (Matthew 13:31–33). The church's early martyrs, by singing hymns on the way to execution, birthed movements that outlived emperors. In modern times, civil-rights activists grounded in biblical justice inspired legislative change far beyond their local congregations. Communities of resistance form when shared spiritual disciplines, like corporate lament and intercessory prayer, braid hearts together against cultural undertow. Daniel undoubtedly prayed with his companions before interpreting Nebuchadnezzar's dream, and that collective dependence became their common backbone. Such solidarity counters the isolation that tyrants and algorithms alike exploit, reminding believers they are members of a body whose Head grants courage. Ripple effects also extend intergenerationally; Daniel's prophecies sustained later exiles returning under Cyrus, and his visions nourished first-century hope of Messiah's kingdom. Mentorship replicates resilience by translating wisdom into the vernacular of younger disciples, turning personal breakthroughs into communal inheritance. Churches that tell conversion stories publicly reinforce the narrative that God still liberates, fueling fresh acts of faith. Digital storytelling offers additional avenues: testimonies livestreamed from living rooms can embolden believers continents away. Yet ripple effects are not restricted to insiders; Nebuchadnezzar and Darius issued empire-wide decrees praising Israel's God in response to Daniel's faithfulness (Daniel 4:34–37; 6:25–27). Such public worship statements demonstrate that resistant communities can reform institutions from within, shaping policy toward justice and mercy. The momentum of these cascading influences compels us to trace Daniel's storyline in detail, for the mechanics of his witness supply a template for contemporary application. Mapping the book's structure will therefore equip readers to follow the narrative's flow and anchor subsequent chapters in exegetical clarity.

1.4 Mapping Daniel's Book for the Journey Ahead

1.4.1 Narrative Court Tales (Chapters 1–6)

Daniel opens with young exiles standing at Nebuchadnezzar's court, confronting food laws that test covenant loyalty while highlighting God's favor in intellectual excellence. The narrative proceeds to chapter 2, where a forgotten dream threatens wholesale execution of wise men, inviting Daniel to prove that divine revelation trumps human clairvoyance. Chapter 3 shifts focus to Daniel's friends, whose furnace ordeal dramatizes the cost of public non-conformity and God's redemptive presence in suffering. Chapter 4 reads like a royal autobiography, portraying Nebuchadnezzar's descent into beast-like madness, a living parable of pride undone until the monarch lifts his eyes to heaven and exalts the Most High. Chapter 5 juxtaposes Belshazzar's blasphemous feast with a disembodied hand that inscribes doom on palace plaster, underscoring how sacrilege accelerates judgment. Chapter 6 introduces Darius's administrative reforms that breed jealousy, culminating in a draconian prayer ban that hurls Daniel into lions' jaws, only for angelic deliverance to vindicate steadfast worship. Each court tale escalates the stakes of allegiance, moving from dietary minutiae to life-or-death edicts, and each episode climaxes in a pagan ruler acknowledging Yahweh's supremacy. The stories weave a pattern: human power rises, confronts divine holiness, is humbled, and ends in praise. Literary artistry surfaces in recursive phrasing—"O king, live forever"—which ironically punctuates narratives proving only God's kingdom endures. These tales also pioneer the Bible's earliest depictions of civil disobedience rooted in worship, informing later apostles who insist on obeying God rather than men (Acts 5:29). Their accumulated momentum prepares readers for visionary sections, assuring that the God who rescues from furnaces and dens also governs cosmic history. Accordingly, the narrative half of Daniel functions as experiential groundwork for the apocalyptic half, establishing credibility for visions that will soon unveil empires yet unborn.

1.4.2 Apocalyptic Visions (Chapters 7–12)

Chapter 7 fractures chronological order, plunging backward to Daniel's dream of four hybrid beasts rising from a stormy sea, images that decode successive empires yet ultimately yield to the everlasting dominion of the Son of Man. Chapter 8 narrows focus to a ram and goat, spotlighting Medo-Persian and Greek eras and forecasting Antiochus IV's desecration of the temple, thereby proving God's foreknowledge of specific tyrants. Chapter 9 intertwines history and liturgy as Daniel's study of Jeremiah's seventy years propels him into confessional prayer, eliciting Gabriel's explanation of seventy sevens that stretch from exile to Messiah's atonement. Chapters 10–12 form a unified revelation, commencing with a river-side Christophany that weakens Daniel's frame yet strengthens his spirit to receive detailed predictions of Persian and Hellenistic intrigues, culminating in eschatological conflict and bodily resurrection. These visions adopt symbolic numerals, cosmic geography, and angelic warfare to unveil temporal cycles through a theological lens. Notably, each vision embeds exhortations to covenant faithfulness, anchoring future hope to present obedience. The Son of Man motif later shapes Jesus' self-designation, forging canonical links that animate New-Testament apocalyptic (Mark 14:62; Revelation 1:13). While beasts terrify, the Ancient of Days enthrones saints, reminding readers that sovereignty never vacates heaven. The visions therefore balance the court tales' concrete deliverances with cosmic panoramas, teaching that divine rescue sometimes occurs within history but always culminates beyond it. Such breadth equips believers to interpret headlines without panic, recognizing that empires rise and fall on Divine timetable. This apocalyptic tapestry invites literary analysis, for its bilingual composition and chiastic structures intensify theological claims, a matter to which we now turn.

1.4.3 Literary Architecture and Languages

Daniel's bilingualism—Hebrew framing Aramaic core—mirrors the book's dual audience: covenant community and surrounding nations. Chapter 1 begins in Hebrew, situating the exile within Israel's redemptive story, but chapter 2 abruptly shifts to Aramaic, the lingua franca of imperial bureaucracy, signaling that divine wisdom addresses public discourse. The Aramaic section extends through chapter 7, forming an intentional chiasm: dream of four kingdoms (2), trial by fire (3), humbling of a king (4), doom of a king (5), trial by lions (6), vision of four kingdoms (7). This literary symmetry highlights God's consistent sovereignty across varied crises, while placing the Ancient of Days vision at the chiastic apex to declare ultimate authority. Chapters 8–12 revert to Hebrew, drawing the covenant community into deeper prophetic reflection on their historical vocation. Interwoven temporal markers—"in the first year," "in the third year"—create a rhythm that contrasts divine chronology with human calendars. Repetition of verbs like "see," "behold," and "understand" signals a progression from sensory experience to spiritual insight. Numerological patterns—seven, seventy, and "time, times, and half a time"—encode theological freight, portraying judgment as measured and mercy as magnified. Angelic dialogues model interpretive humility, reminding readers that apocalyptic requires revelation, not speculation. The book's closing command to Daniel, "Go your way until the end" (12:13), functions as structural bookend to chapter 1's exile, framing the whole narrative as faithful pilgrimage. Recognizing these literary features prevents reductionist reading and guides responsible exposition, which is crucial for the methodological framework presented next.

1.5 Method and Framework for This Book

1.5.1 Historical-Grammatical and Canonical Readings

Sound interpretation begins by situating Daniel within sixth-century Babylon while acknowledging later editorial shaping that preserved the text for post-exilic audiences. Archaeological data about Nebuchadnezzar's building campaigns and diplomatic correspondences corroborate the book's imperial atmosphere, anchoring stories in verifiable context. Grammatical analysis of Aramaic verb stems and Hebrew participles exposes narrative pacing and rhetorical emphasis, such as the waw-consecutive pattern that heightens tension in the lion's-den account. Paying attention to genre—court narrative versus apocalyptic vision—guards against flattening distinct literary conventions. Canonically, Daniel functions as hinge between former prophets and apocalyptic literature, echoing Joseph's dream interpretation while prefiguring Revelation's beast imagery. Inter-textual echoes—like the borrowing of Jeremiah's seventy-year prophecy—illustrate how scripture interprets scripture, inviting the reader into a dialogical approach rather than isolated proof-texting. The historical-grammatical method also respects the text's original recipients, who needed assurance that exile had not nullified covenant promises. Yet responsible exegesis never stops at ancient horizons; it travels forward through canonical linkage so that the Son of Man's vindication informs Christian hope. This dual lens—historical specificity and canonical coherence—will underpin every chapter that follows, ensuring that application flows from sound exposition rather than creative extrapolation. With these safeguards in place, the study can explore theological themes that thread through Daniel and modern discipleship alike.

1.5.2 Theological Themes Lens

Sovereignty emerges as the book's melodic line, asserting that God rules kingdoms and calendars, turning human hubris into doxology. Holiness surfaces as harmony, manifested in dietary distinctiveness, prayer discipline, and ethical courage, all pointing toward the cruciform purity fulfilled in Christ. Exile forms the rhythmic beat, reminding believers they are resident aliens whose primary citizenship lies in heaven (Philippians 3:20). Revelation supplies orchestration, unveiling hidden realities so that present obedience draws strength from future certainty. Kingdom contrast fleshes out the conflict between beastly regimes and the human-yet-divine Son of Man, inviting the church to embody the latter's servant kingship. Suffering and deliverance alternate as counterpoint; sometimes God closes lions' mouths, at other times saints conquer by dying (Revelation 12:11), yet both outcomes testify to His lordship. Prayer integrates these motifs, functioning as theological hinge where sovereignty meets human responsibility. Angels and demons appear not to spark fascination with hierarchies but to affirm that earth's battles mirror cosmic realities, thus dignifying righteous choices. Justice thread runs beneath the narrative, promising that weighed and wanting empires will be replaced by everlasting righteousness (Daniel 7:27). Hope, therefore, is not passive optimism but active alignment with God's unfolding dominion. Tracing these themes provides scaffolding for practical outworking in diverse vocations, a task envisioned by the praxis matrix that now follows.

1.5.3 Praxis Matrix for Contemporary Application

To translate Daniel's ancient witness into modern discipleship, this book proposes four intersecting arenas where counter-cultural faith must take root. Personal devotion cultivates interior resilience through fixed-hour prayer, Scripture meditation, and disciplined rest, echoing Daniel's thrice-daily petitions. Vocational integrity calls believers to integrate excellence and ethics, viewing their craft as liturgy that proclaims God's artistry amid secular metrics. Civic engagement invites participation in policymaking, advocacy, and neighborhood welfare, balancing Jeremiah's call to seek city shalom with prophetic critique of injustice. Prophetic critique encompasses public truth-telling that unmasks idols, whether economic exploitation or digital surveillance, coupling denunciation with gospel invitation. Each arena interacts with the others; robust devotion fuels vocational steadfastness, which lends credibility to civic engagement, which in turn clarifies prophetic speech. Spiritual disciplines serve as trellis for these arenas, ensuring growth is guided rather than haphazard. Accountability structures—small groups, mentoring triads, and ecclesial oversight—prevent lone-ranger activism and foster communal discernment. Failure does not disqualify but becomes material for repentance, reinforcing the gospel's gracious foundation. Cultural intelligence tools help believers exegete societal narratives, discerning where to affirm common grace and where to confront rebellion. The matrix thus equips readers to craft contextual strategies rather than importing one-size-fits-all formulas. Implementing these practices will be facilitated by learning tools explicitly designed for personal and group interaction.

1.5.4 Learning Tools

Each chapter concludes with reflection questions that probe comprehension, surface emotional responses, and prompt actionable next steps, moving readers from insight to implementation. Suggested spiritual practices—such as a media fast aligned with Daniel's dietary resolve—offer concrete exercises for embodying counter-cultural rhythms. Group discussion guides include leader notes that balance open-ended dialogue with doctrinal guardrails, preventing conversations from drifting into speculative tangents. QR codes in the print edition and hyperlinks in the digital version connect readers to supplemental videos, printable prayer liturgies, and curated articles on relevant cultural issues. A glossary clarifies technical terms, from "apocalyptic" to "chiastic structure," ensuring accessibility for lay readers without diluting scholarly rigor. Margin callouts highlight cross-references, allowing quick comparison of Danielic themes with New-Testament passages. An annotated bibliography points toward commentaries, historical monographs, and contemporary essays for deeper study, inviting lifelong learning rather than mere consumption of this volume. Progress trackers enable small groups to celebrate milestones, reinforcing perseverance. For churches, sermon outlines and slide templates simplify integration into preaching calendars, ensuring congregational synergy. Finally, a concluding benediction at the end of each chapter directs hearts toward worship, reminding learners that study aims at adoration. With these tools in place, readers are now prepared to journey into Daniel's lived experience of exile beginning in Chapter 2, carrying with them a robust framework for walking against the world with holy confidence.

1.6 Spiritual Disciplines That Sustain Resistance

1.6.1 Fixed-Hour Prayer

Daniel's refusal to abandon his thrice-daily petitions in the face of a royal decree reminds readers that structured prayer is less a legalistic routine than a survival rhythm that re-centers the heart on God's throne each time culture demands hurried allegiance (Daniel 6:10). Establishing set moments—morning praise, midday intercession, evening examen—interrupts the empire's constant push for productivity by carving out islands of attentiveness in the sea of noise. These pauses soak the imagination in the reality that every breath ultimately belongs to the Ancient of Days, not to corporate deadlines or social approval. Fixed-hour prayer builds within believers a liturgical backbone so that spontaneous prayer flows more freely, just as practiced musicians improvise from muscle memory. The Psalter offers appointed words when personal vocabulary falters; reciting Psalm 55:17, which echoes Daniel's cadence of "evening, morning, and noon," allies contemporary voices with centuries of saints. Setting digital reminders or pairing prayers with daily habits—coffee brewing, lunch break, sunset—integrates liturgy with life, ensuring that devotion is woven, not tacked on. Over time the body itself becomes a timekeeper; hearts quicken with expectancy moments before the next scheduled encounter, mirroring the Israelites who waited for daily manna. Fixed-hour prayers also calibrate emotional equilibrium, letting lament surface at midday rather than festering until nightfall, and letting gratitude close the day instead of anxiety. When friends or colleagues witness these consistent pauses, curiosity can ripen into conversations about the God who listens. Families can adopt the pattern, forming children's memories around table blessings that mature into lifelong habits. Workplace believers might gather briefly in stairwells or conference rooms, sanctifying secular spaces with whispered doxology. In persecuted contexts, synchronized but silent prayer times create invisible fellowship across prison cells and hidden house gatherings. The discipline teaches believers to number their days, as Moses prayed, framing each segment of daylight as stewardship, not entitlement (Psalm 90:12). Because these moments tether human schedules to divine chronology, they naturally widen the soul's capacity to carry the burdens of others, which ushers the community into the practice of corporate lament and confession that follows.

1.6.2 Corporate Lament and Confession

If fixed-hour prayer trains individual hearts, corporate lament knits those hearts into a resilient fabric capable of absorbing communal grief without tearing. Daniel's intercessory confession on behalf of the exiled nation in chapter 9 exemplifies how one person's contrition can catalyze a collective return to covenant fidelity. Modern worship often rushes to celebratory choruses, but exile-shaped spirituality insists that honest sorrow precedes durable hope. Lament congregations give language to systemic sin, whether racial injustice, ecological exploitation, or habitual consumerism, refusing to sanitize anguish with shallow clichés. Confession shifts blame from nebulous "culture" to shared complicity, echoing Nehemiah's inclusive phrasing—"we have acted very corruptly" (Nehemiah 1:7). When believers read penitential psalms antiphonally, they declare that grace addresses communities, not just isolated individuals. The practice dismantles performative piety by making vulnerability normative, allowing leaders to model repentance rather than curate perfection. Tears shed together dissolve the myth of self-sufficiency and invite the Spirit's comfort promised to mourners (Matthew 5:4). Churches that weave lament into liturgy discover that visitors bearing hidden wounds recognize a safe harbor where pain is neither trivialized nor weaponized. Confessional gatherings also tutor theological imagination, showing that divine justice and mercy are not competing attributes but interlocking facets of holy love. Intercessory confession for civic corruption—mirroring Daniel's plea for Jerusalem—awakens congregations to vocation as spiritual priests for their cities (1 Peter 2:9). When lament culminates in absolution, the gospel's sweetness deepens because the bitterness of sin has been tasted collectively. Celebration that erupts afterward rings truer, for joy rises like a dawn that knows the night. This shared journey through sorrow forges solidarity strong enough to withstand external hostility, setting the stage for embodied practices such as fasting that transform inner contrition into visible protest.

1.6.3 Fasting as Protest Against Empire

Fasting stands at the crossroads of worship and witness, declaring with the body that ultimate satisfaction is found in God, not in the empire's buffet of delights. Daniel's initial vegetable diet functioned as a partial fast, quietly subverting the king's hospitality that sought to entice loyalty by palate (Daniel 1:8). Biblical prophets fasted to amplify prayers for justice, and Jesus assumed His followers would do likewise when He said, "When you fast" (Matthew 6:16-18). In a culture obsessed with food aesthetics and instant gratification, voluntarily foregoing meals communicates a counter-narrative that humans thrive not by bread alone but by every word from God's mouth (Deuteronomy 8:3). Fasting sharpens spiritual perception; as physical hunger surfaces, it echoes creation's groan for redemption, prompting intercession for those whose poverty forces involuntary hunger. Acts of abstinence can extend beyond food—digital fasts interrupt algorithms, financial fasts curb consumerism, and noise fasts reclaim silence from entertainment empires. Corporate fasts unite congregations around crises such as trafficking, war, or legislation that threatens religious liberty, aligning appetites with heaven's priorities. Historically, movements for societal change—from Nineveh's repentance (Jonah 3:5-10) to civil-rights advocacy—have paired fasting with public action, signaling moral urgency. When believers donate saved meal money to relief efforts, fasting becomes a concrete channel for generosity, fulfilling Isaiah 58's vision of a fast that looses injustice. The discipline also detoxes the soul from dependency on caffeine, sugar, or scrolling, making space for scripture to taste sweeter than honey. Physical weakness experienced during fasts exposes idols of productivity and forces reliance on Spirit strength, an echo of Paul's boast in weakness (2 Corinthians 12:9). Fasting prepares the heart for feasting by restoring gratitude; ordinary bread after a fast becomes sacrament, reminding eaters of manna's miracle. Because fasting engages both body and imagination, it primes believers to receive scripture not as mere information but as a living drama in which they participate, guiding the transition to meditative practices that cultivate apocalyptic vision.

1.6.4 Scripture Meditation and Apocalyptic Imagination

Meditation is the art of slow attendance to God's speech until its cadence syncs with the heartbeat, and the book of Daniel invites such lingering because its layered symbols yield fruit only to patient gazing. Unlike hurried proof-texting, biblical meditation resembles Mary treasuring words in her heart, turning phrases over until light refracts from every angle (Luke 2:19). Rehearsing Daniel's portrait of the Son of Man ascending to the Ancient of Days trains the mind to see present headlines through the lens of a coming, unshakeable kingdom. Apocalyptic texts expand the sanctified imagination; they teach believers to decode beastly propaganda and to anticipate resurrection, galvanizing courage to act justly in the interim. Lectio divina methods—read, reflect, respond, rest—can guide engagement, allowing verses to question assumptions rather than vice versa. Visualizing the stone that topples the statue (Daniel 2:34-35) fuels hope that unseen seeds of righteousness will one day fill the earth, an antidote to despair amid cultural decline. Memorizing short passages equips disciples to confront temptation much as Jesus quoted Deuteronomy in the wilderness. Artistic response—journaling, poetry, or icon sketching—embeds the Word in multiple neural pathways, enhancing recall under pressure. Group meditation sessions foster communal discernment; diverse insights surface, correcting private misreadings and echoing the early church's collective devotion to apostolic teaching (Acts 2:42). Digital tools can serve rather than distract when believers curate playlists of dramatized scripture or set lock-screen verses that greet every phone unlock. Meditation also inoculates against sensational end-times speculation by grounding interpretation in worship, not anxiety. As believers carve reflective silence into routines, they hear whispers of vocation that align spiritual gifts with tangible needs in their neighborhoods. The Spirit often pairs meditation with creative mission ideas, illustrating that contemplation and action are dance partners, not rivals. Over time scripture-saturated imaginations produce spontaneous prayer that sounds like prophecy, because hearts overflow with God's vocabulary. This cycle completes the suite of disciplines in Chapter 1, launching readers into the narrative world of Chapter 2 with souls attuned, appetites disciplined, and imaginations captivated—ready to walk against the world alongside Daniel and his companions.

Conclusion

The story of Daniel beckons us beyond abstract piety into a vibrant faith that refuses to conform, yet neither shrinks from compassionate engagement. His journey underlines a timeless truth: every act of obedience, however hidden, feeds the momentum of gospel witness. He teaches that holiness is less a list of dos and don'ts than a dynamic allegiance rooted in prayer, shaped by Scripture, and expressed through courageous service. As we close this opening chapter, we stand reminded that counter-cultural living is not reserved for extraordinary figures alone but is the calling of every believer empowered by the same Spirit who raised Christ from the dead (Romans 8:11).

Moving forward, we will accompany Daniel into the crucible of exile, where identity-tested choices will forge resilience for the tasks ahead. Our exploration will continue, not as detached observers of a distant past, but as co-heirs of God's promises—challenge-ready, hope-anchored, and mission-driven. Let the patterns we have uncovered here take root: let prayer become our anchor, Scripture our roadmap, conviction our banner, and community our fortress. In doing so, we will walk against the world not with stubborn defiance, but with the joyful confidence that, in every age, the One who calls us remains supremely worthy of our fidelity.

Chapter 2 – Exile and Identity: Daniel's Early Tests

The experience of exile reshapes every facet of life—home becomes unfamiliar, rituals lose their former resonance, and core identities are pressed against the pressures of a dominant culture. Daniel and his companions entered Babylonian society as uprooted youths, carrying the weight of a destroyed temple and a fractured promise. Yet in the crucible of forced displacement, they discovered that true belonging rests not in geography or bloodline but in unwavering devotion to the living God. Their response to renaming ceremonies, re-education programs, and gastronomic enticements reveals faith's power to redefine tribal loyalty and intellectual ambition. By refusing to capitulate at the king's table, recalibrating their schedules around prayer, and forging bonds of mutual support, these young exiles laid the groundwork for a resilient identity—one that no imperial decree could dismantle. As we explore their early trials, we will see how every test served to clarify what mattered most and to fortify the convictions that would sustain them through palace intrigues and fiery furnaces.

2.0 Setting the Stage—From Jerusalem's Ashes to Babylon's Gates

The fall of Jerusalem in 605 BC marked a traumatic turning point in Israel's history, shattering centuries of national confidence and uprooting people whose lives had revolved around temple ritual and

Davidic kingship. As Babylonian forces swept through Judah, deportation caravans carried away artisans, soldiers, and young nobles alike, severing families from ancestral land and sacred shrine. The devastation was not only physical but theological: with the temple desecrated and the ark absent, Israel's worship life was abruptly suspended. Prophetic voices like Jeremiah had long warned of this inevitability, yet experiencing the siege's horrors in real time pressed the community to wrestle with a God who allowed His own city to be razed (Jeremiah 25:8-11). The shockwave of loss reverberated in laments that still echo in Psalm 137, where exiles hung their harps on willow trees rather than offer music to captors who jeered their God. Even as hope flickered in prophecies of eventual return (Isaiah 40; Ezekiel 37), the immediate reality was one of disorientation: Babylon loomed as a superpower whose gods had proven superior to Yahweh's temple defenses. This imperial ascendancy was reinforced by Nebuchadnezzar's lavish building projects, which showcased Babylon's architectural and military might, offering exiles an unspoken invitation to transfer loyalty from the God of Zion to the gods of Babylon. Political alliances in Jerusalem were exposed as feeble alliances of convenience, illustrating that human covenants crumble when weighed against imperial agendas. In this vacuum of broken promises, identity itself became fluid, threatening to dissolve into the cosmopolitan milieu of Babylon's multicultural court. Yet even amid rubble and exile, seeds of resilient faith took root, nurtured by memories of Sinai covenant and whispered Torah readings among displaced families. Communities began meeting in homes for portable liturgies, anticipating the synagogue model that would flourish in later centuries. These emerging practices kept alive the hope that Yahweh's presence was not confined to a building, but accompanied His people wherever they went (Ezekiel 11:16-17). Into this fraught context stepped Daniel and his companions, chosen for their promise yet destined to face tests that would redefine their sense of self. Their story begins where Jerusalem ended, illustrating how God's purposes transcend destroyed shrines and depopulated cities. The unfolding chapters will trace how deportation trauma intersected with personal conviction, setting the stage for identity forged not in comfort but in exile.

2.1 The Trauma of Deportation

2.1.1 Displacement and Disorientation

For Daniel and his peers, the journey from Jerusalem to Babylon was not merely a change of address but a rupture of every familiar horizon. The caravan's slow pace through desert landscapes magnified anxiety, as exiles trudged alongside armed guards who reminded them of their powerlessness. Separation from family networks compounded the anguish, leaving young nobles without elders to teach the stories of patriarchs or recite Yahweh's promises around hearth fires. Language barriers accentuated isolation, for Aramaic idioms and courtly jargon sounded strange on lips used to Hebrew prayers. Each night under alien stars heightened the sense of cosmic dislocation: the heavens that once bore witness to Davidic kingship now presided over captivity. Questions swirled: Did God still inhabit Babylon's soil? Had He abandoned His covenant people? Such theological disorientation paralleled physical vulnerability, as exiles grappled with reduced rations, sun-scorched roads, and disease. Historical records suggest that Babylonian deportation policy aimed to prevent uprisings by uprooting elites, a strategy that left communities feeling decapitated. Without priests to offer sacrifices, communal worship pivoted to memory and song, yet even these disciplines risked fading under constant stress. In this maelstrom of fear and loss, the instinct to assimilate for mere survival tempted many to abandon distinctive practices. Some exiles likely adopted Babylonian names and gods out of desperation, hoping that compromise might secure mercy from imperial authorities. Others withdrew into insular cliques, seeking comfort in narrow enclaves rather than trusting adaptation under God's unseen hand. Yet the very extremity of displacement also opened space for radical trust in divine promises that transcended geography. Prophetic fragments treasured in exilic circles—Jeremiah's assurances of restoration, Ezekiel's visions of returning glory—offered glimmers of hope that identity could endure beyond walls of stone. This complex interplay of fear, adaptation, and hope paved the way for Daniel's first conscious choice to resist assimilation, a choice grounded in theological clarity that we now turn to explore.

2.1.2 Loss of Temple-Centered Worship

The temple in Jerusalem had been more than a building; it stood as the focal point of Israel's covenantal relationship with Yahweh. Priests had daily offered sacrifices, and festivals had drawn families from every tribe to remember deliverance from Egypt and covenant renewal at Sinai. With the temple razed and vessels carried off to Babylon, Israel's liturgical heartbeat faltered. Without altar fires or Levitical choirs, exiles resorted to mnemonic worship—reciting Torah passages in cramped quarters or singing psalms by heart. The trauma of ritual suspension cut to the core of communal identity: if worship ceased, did Israel remain the people of God? Jeremiah's lament for the shrine echoed in exile when he acknowledged that homemade laments could not fully replace temple rites (Lamentations 2). Ezekiel's poignant vision of God's glory departing the temple (Ezekiel 10) foreshadowed exile's darkness, yet also foreshadowed God's eventual promise to gather His scattered flock (Ezekiel 34). As the priestly system lay dormant, lay leaders and scribes assumed roles of guidance, preserving Torah in alternative loci of encounter—homes, street corners, informal gatherings. This shift democratized access to scripture, planting seeds for post-exilic reforms that emphasized study alongside sacrifice. Daniel himself, trained in royal courts, would draw upon these portable worship models to sustain prayer life without temple infrastructure (Daniel 6:10). The loss of centralized worship forced a reevaluation of where God's presence truly resided: not in stones and vessels, but in hearts attuned to His voice. This insight would prove vital when Daniel interpreted dreams: his authority derived not from ritual office but from personal communion with the Living God. As we consider how internal rhythms replaced external forms, we gain perspective on how identity anchored in worship can survive even when historic sanctuaries lie in ruins. The exile's recalibration of temple dependence consequently shapes our own reimagining of divine presence amid disrupted traditions.

2.1.3 Prophetic Frameworks for Suffering

Ancient prophets did not merely forecast doom; they provided pastoral scaffolding for exiles to endure suffering with theological integrity. Jeremiah's letter to the first deportees instructed them to build houses, plant gardens, and seek the welfare of Babylon, for their captivity would span decades (Jeremiah 29:4-7). This counsel reframed exile from a purely punitive stage to a season of purposeful presence, requiring commitment to host culture's stability without capitulating to its idolatry. Ezekiel, taken in the second wave of deportation, received visions by the Kebar River that portrayed God's mobility—His glory leaving the temple but going with the people (Ezekiel 1:1-3; 11:22-23). These visions assured exiles that no geographical displacement could sever covenant ties, as Yahweh's throne was not rooted in stone but accompanied His faithful anywhere. Prophetic drama acted as both warning and promise: enactment of symbolic signs—lying on one side, shaving hair—illustrated the communal cost of unrepentance (Ezekiel 4:4-8), yet also signaled the hope of purification and restoration once the required period of judgment passed. Minor prophets like Habakkuk voiced raw lament over violence and injustice but concluded that the righteous live by faith, a maxim that would sustain communities under foreign rule (Habakkuk 2:4). These prophetic frameworks did not eliminate pain but provided narrative anchors—promises to recall when despair threatened to erase identity. They taught exiles to interpret suffering as part of a larger redemptive drama, positioning their hardship within a timeline that included future vindication. Daniel, steeped in such prophetic milieu, internalized this theology of endurance, enabling him to pray with bold confession in chapter 9 and to stand firm under imperial decrees. Understanding these prophetic antecedents clarifies how Daniel's early tests were not isolated events but chapters in God's unfolding story of judgement and hope. With this theological backdrop, we now examine the finer mechanisms of exile designed to reshape identity through renaming and re-education.

2.2 Renaming and Re-education

2.2.1 The Politics of Names

Names in the ancient Near East carried deep significance, functioning as verbal identity cards that conveyed lineage, allegiance, and destiny. When Babylon's officials renamed Daniel and his companions, they performed an act of symbolic conquest, attempting to sever ties to covenant heritage. Daniel, originally meaning "God is my judge," became Belteshazzar, a title invoking the Babylonian god Bel's protection over the king. Hananiah ("Yahweh is gracious") was rechristened Shadrach, alluding to the moon god Aku, while Mishael ("Who is what God is?") became Meshach, and Azariah ("Yahweh helps") took the name Abednego. Each new name functioned as a subtle catechism, drilling foreign deities into the minds of these youths. The pattern echoed Babel's earlier ambition to unify humanity under a single linguistic banner (Genesis 11:1-9), reinforcing imperial propaganda that loyalty to the state's gods merited security. Yet names cannot erase internal convictions, and Daniel's refusal to answer to Belteshazzar demonstrated that confession of divine identity transcends bureaucratic labels. Modern parallels emerge when organizations require employees to adopt brand-centric email aliases or avatars that align personal identity with corporate image. Such renaming mechanisms, while less dramatic than ancient edicts, still aim to shape self-conception. Daniel's example encourages believers to resist internalizing external labels that conflict with God-given identity, rejecting any nomenclature that would redefine their primary allegiance. Recognizing the politics of naming helps contemporary disciples safeguard vocations—whether in professional titles, social media handles, or academic credentials—from covert attempts at theological reprogramming. In doing so, they echo Daniel's bold stance: preserving the name of Yahweh on lips and hearts even when official registers declare otherwise.

2.2.2 Curriculum of the Chaldeans

Beyond renaming, Babylonian authorities enrolled young exiles in an intensive three-year curriculum designed to produce civil servants steeped in imperial ideology. The program covered Chaldean language and literature, mathematics for fiscal administration, astrology for divination, omen texts for decision-making, and legal codes for judicial service. This education aimed not merely at skill acquisition but at worldview formation—teaching that celestial patterns governed human affairs and that devotion to Nebuchadnezzar's court gods ensured cosmic favor. Classical texts preserved in Nineveh profiles attest to similar schools in other Mesopotamian capitals, underscoring a standardized approach to assimilation through academic excellence. To excel in this program was to gain social mobility, but at the cost of internalizing values antithetical to Israel's covenant ethic. Daniel's proficiency in these disciplines earned him and his friends places at the royal table, yet he navigated the curriculum without surrendering spiritual distinctiveness. He absorbed the tools of administration while filtering them through the prism of Torah truth. This adaptive posture offers a model for modern believers in professional training programs that prize cultural conformity—medicine, law, business, and even seminary contexts. The task is to master competencies without compromising conviction, using secular expertise as a platform for kingdom witness. Recognizing the hidden curriculum—the implicit values conveyed through textbooks, assessments, and institutional rituals—is the first step toward discerning which elements to appropriate and which to repudiate. Daniel's example shows that academic success need not equate to spiritual sale-out; rather, excellence can underscore God's generative creativity and justice. As we assess the implications of such re-education efforts, we turn next to principles for negotiating cultural literacy under exile conditions.

2.2.3 Negotiating Cultural Literacy

Engaging with dominant cultural systems demands more than passive exposure; it requires active discernment to differentiate between neutral knowledge and worldview-laden ideology. Daniel's mastery of Aramaic and Chaldean science provided him with credibility at court, yet he never allowed that credibility to supplant his identity as a covenant child. He consumed the empire's culture as a means to an end—gaining access for the gospel of Yahweh—rather than as an end in itself. In contemporary terms, this translates to cultivating "double listening": hearing secular narratives on their own terms while interpreting them through biblical categories. For example, studying psychology or economics can enhance ministry and workplace effectiveness, but reliance on theories that deny human dignity or absolute moral truth must be resisted. Daniel's approach underscores the importance of setting bookmarks in one's mental library—flagging concepts that require theological critique alongside those that can be redeemed for kingdom purposes. This practice also involves forming learning communities, where peers can engage in rigorous dialogue about course content and its spiritual implications. Accountability partners serve as sounding boards, helping to detect subtle shifts in allegiance that often accompany prolonged immersion in secular environments. Technology offers tools like collaborative note-sharing and virtual study groups, enabling believers to cultivate counter-narratives even when physically separated. Writing marginalia in textbooks or maintaining reflection journals transforms passive reception into active engagement, ensuring that scriptural truth remains the interpretive lens. Daniel's theological acumen, demonstrated when he discerned the king's dream significance, emerged from such reflective habits. Ultimately, negotiating cultural literacy means refusing to let any body of knowledge become an idol; instead, all learning is offered back to God as an act of worship (Romans 12:2). This posture equips exiles in every era to serve with integrity, leveraging cultural insights for redemptive service rather than capitulative conformity.

2.3 The Food Test—Table Fellowship as Theological Boundary

2.3.1 Ritual Purity and Royal Provisions

Daniel and his three friends faced a daily dilemma when the royal steward brought them meat and wine from the king's table, provisions likely offered to Babylonian deities as part of imperial liturgies (Daniel 1:5). Consuming these foods would have violated Mosaic dietary laws that distinguished clean from unclean animals and prohibited fellowship with foreign idols (Leviticus 11; Deuteronomy 14). Beyond technical prohibition, the issue signified deeper loyalty: eating the king's food symbolized acceptance of Babylon's gods and a repudiation of covenant faithfulness. The banquets were imbued with propaganda, teaching that allegiance to Nebuchadnezzar's table guaranteed health, prosperity, and favor, just as Israelite festivals had trained God's people to associate obedience with blessing (Deuteronomy 28). Daniel's abstention thus functioned as a protest against equating divine blessing with imperial largesse. The steward Ashpenaz, uncertain how to handle their refusal, faced political risk in denying his master's orders, illustrating that dietary resistance had cascading repercussions for entire households. The narrative emphasizes that holiness often begins with hidden choices, formed in the silence of kitchens far from palaces. In a world where food could be weaponized as soft power, Daniel's stand transforms the mundane act of eating into a sacred boundary marker. Modern parallels emerge in settings where workplace perks implicitly demand compromise—company-sponsored retreats that feature morally questionable entertainment, or client dinners that pressure professionals to drink excessively. Just as Daniel weighed his belly against his soul's obedience, contemporary believers must discern when seemingly neutral benefits mask ideological demands. The steward's eventual acquiescence to their request reveals how consistent integrity can reshape power dynamics, demonstrating that refusal can invite negotiation rather than mere punishment. By situating ritual purity at the heart of table fellowship, Daniel's experience teaches that the body itself is a theological frontier where identity is either reinforced or eroded. This realization prepares us to consider how courage and creativity combined in their proposal to the steward, forming the next step in solidifying their exile identity.

2.3.2 Courageous Request and Creative Compromise

Rather than mounting a frontal assault on Babylonian practice, Daniel employed diplomatic tact by proposing a ten-day trial of vegetables and water, asking Ashpenaz to judge their appearance and health afterward (Daniel 1:12–13). This approach balanced firm conviction with respectful dialogue, illustrating that standing against cultural norms need not resort to abrasive tactics. By suggesting a limited testing period, Daniel reframed the conflict as an empirical investigation rather than outright defiance, thereby reducing the steward's fear of reprisal and opening space for compromise. This creative strategy showcases wisdom in navigating hostile environments: principled yet pragmatic, it invites opponents to witness the fruit of obedience firsthand. Their willingness to submit to evaluation undercut assumptions that godly diets would produce weakness or ill health. In proposing a diet consistent with their heritage—vegetables symbolizing soil and life—Daniel spotlighted God's sustaining power over manufactured imperial provisions. The steward's cooperation for ten days signaled that even systems designed for total control contain points of pressure where integrity can effect change. This dynamic resonates for believers in secular institutions who advocate for ethical adjustments—such as scheduling prayer times or accommodating sabbath rest—without alienating leadership. It reminds us that negotiating for faithful practice often involves naming a limited request, demonstrating its viability, and building trust through results. The ten-day trial also underscores the importance of temporal framing: by avoiding open-ended abstinence, Daniel minimized risk and secured a controlled environment in which God's favor could be displayed. His example encourages thoughtful engagement tactics: approaching cultural gatekeepers with proposals they can evaluate fairly rather than abstract demands they can dismiss as fanaticism. As their trial concluded, the visible impact on body and mind forced a reappraisal of assumptions, paving the way for lasting policy changes. This interplay of courage and creativity thus prepares the ground for reflecting on the tangible outcomes that confirmed God's blessing.

2.3.3 Outcomes: Healthier Bodies, Sharper Minds

At the end of the ten-day period, the steward observed that Daniel and his friends appeared healthier and more robust than those who consumed royal rations, prompting him to continue their diet (Daniel 1:15). This outcome vindicated their convictions, showing that divine blessing can confound worldly expectations when obedience is rooted in genuine faith rather than ritualism. Physical vitality became a signboard pointing to God's custodial care, disrupting the association between imperial provision and ultimate security. Their freedom from idolatrous rites did not result in marginalization but in elevated status—Daniel and his companions outperformed peers in wisdom and understanding, leading "in every matter of wisdom and understanding" (Daniel 1:20). This dual flourishing of body and mind affirms that covenant loyalty yields holistic well-being, a principle the apostle Paul echoes when he calls the body a temple of the Holy Spirit (1 Corinthians 6:19-20). The narrative reveals that God's diet—life-giving and wise—nourishes more than digestion; it sharpens cognitive abilities and moral insight. In Babylon, where astrology and logic were prized, their exceptional performance signaled that Israel's God imparted superior revelation. This dynamic mirrors modern studies showing that lifestyle choices grounded in disciplined values produce better mental health, reinforcing the link between spiritual practices and intellectual flourishing. The story also highlights that success in resisting cultural norms can generate opportunities for influence: as Daniel advanced in the court, he gained a platform for further acts of faithful interpretation. The steward's decision to adopt their dietary regimen speaks to the contagious potential of integrity when backed by tangible results. By refusing compromise on minor matters, Daniel and his friends prevented incremental erosion of deeper convictions. Their experience affirms that prudent non-conformity, when combined with excellence, can reframe entire systems, inviting observers to question prevailing paradigms. As we transition from this decisive test, we move into broader patterns of identity formation, examining how such early stands informed ongoing practices and communal postures in exile.

2.4 Identity Formation in Exile: Practices and Postures

2.4.1 Faithful Presence vs Strategic Withdrawal

Exile posed the dilemma of whether to isolate in insular enclaves or to engage richly in Babylonian society while maintaining distinctiveness. Jeremiah's counsel to "seek the welfare of the city" (Jeremiah 29:7) legitimized active participation in civic life despite absence of the temple, yet prophets also decried idolatry and compromise (Ezekiel 8). Daniel navigated this tension by serving in high governmental offices while preserving covenantal convictions, demonstrating that faithful presence involves both contribution and critique. His approach avoided two extremes—ghettoization that forfeits public influence and assimilation that relinquishes theological integrity. Instead, he exemplified a posture of "in but not of," aligning with Jesus' teaching that disciples are "in the world" but not "of the world" (John 17:14-16). Faithful presence meant mastering Babylonian protocols—language, law, ceremony—so as to bring wisdom and justice informed by Torah ethics. Yet strategic withdrawal surfaced when policies demanded idolatrous compliance, as with required offerings at royal banquets, at which point he abstained rather than conform. This calibrated engagement protected his ability to act as a credible insider without becoming captive to cultural norms. Contemporary believers face similar choices in workplaces and social circles: when to build bridges through shared initiatives and when to draw clear lines refusing complicity in unethical practices. The posture of faithful presence challenges isolationism by affirming that God's mission unfolds amid complexity, not solely within church walls. It also rejects naïve activism that sacrifices spiritual rootedness for social acceptance. Daniel's balanced engagement invites modern disciples to develop discernment for where authentic ministry can thrive and where conscience demands principled distance, ensuring that exile identity remains both visible and uncompromised. This dynamic interplay between participation and refusal sets the stage for vocational excellence as a form of witness.

2.4.2 Vocational Excellence as Witness

Daniel's exemplary performance in administrative tasks, dream interpretation, and policy advice earned him promotions under successive monarchs, illustrating that vocational skillfulness can itself serve as a form of gospel proclamation. His nine times greater wisdom, compared to seasoned Babylonians, functioned not as self-glorification but as a testimony to Yahweh's unrivaled wisdom (Daniel 1:20). This principle aligns with the apostolic injunction in Colossians to work heartily as for the Lord rather than for men (Colossians 3:23). Excellence in one's craft communicates respect for the common good and stewardship of God-given talents, opening doors for deeper conversations about ultimate allegiance. Daniel's unwillingness to exploit insider knowledge for personal gain further bolstered his credibility, for integrity in public administration became a rare commodity in imperial courts known for bribery and nepotism. His balanced judgment in court cases and fiscal matters revealed that biblical ethics can inform public policy and corporate governance alike. The impact of such exemplary service ripples outward: colleagues gain confidence that just rule can coexist with efficiency, and subordinates learn that competence and conscience need not clash. Modern believers in professions ranging from medicine to education can similarly integrate technical proficiency with ethical standards drawn from scripture. Pursuing excellence must be paired with humility, echoing Daniel's constant deference to God as the true source of insight. This vocational witness also involves mentoring younger colleagues, modeling servant leadership that prizes the flourishing of others above self-promotion. When decisions prioritize justice, equity, and compassion, the workplace becomes a platform for kingdom values. As we examine how vocational faithfulness bolsters communal identity, we turn next to the formation of covenant communities amid exile's adversity.

2.4.3 Covenant Community in Hostile Spaces

Isolation makes resistance unsustainable, yet in exile, forming communities often entailed hidden gatherings and coded rituals to avoid imperial detection. Daniel likely connected with fellow exiles for mutual encouragement, drawing upon synagogue prototypes where Torah was read aloud and psalms intoned (Nehemiah 8:1-8). Shared liturgies preserved theological identity, forming a counterculture within a dominant empire. Storytelling about patriarchs and prophets functioned as mnemonic rehearsals of covenant history, reinforcing group solidarity and hope for restoration. Accountability networks helped detect drift toward assimilation, as peers could gently correct one another when compromises crept in. Sabbath celebrations, though perhaps adjusted for captivity conditions, sustained rhythm of divine sovereignty over human schedules. Covenantal meals—simple fare echoing Passover—reminded participants of God's deliverance beyond Babylon's bread. Prayer cells, meeting in private homes or behind palace walls before morning petitions, paralleled Daniel's solo prayers but added communal resonance. Such communities also engaged in acts of compassion toward needy exiles and even hospitable gestures toward sympathetic Babylonians, modeling gospel hospitality (Hebrews 13:2). Intergenerational bonds, with elders passing on Torah truths to youth, prevented loss of identity across cohorts. Artistic expressions—psalm paraphrases set to local melodies—blended cultural forms with sacred content, enabling worship that was contextual yet distinct. These communities served as spiritual incubators, equipping members to bear witness individually and corporately. In our context, forming covenant communities may involve small groups, online forums, or interchurch networks that prioritize shared disciplines and mutual accountability. As Daniel's early stands reveal, identity strengthened in community sustains the solitary tests that inevitably lie ahead. With these practices and postures mapped, we now turn to contemporary parallels, exploring how modern exiles navigate analogous pressures in today's "Babylons."

2.5 Contemporary Parallels—Exile at the Office, Campus, and Online

2.5.1 Exile in Corporate Cultures

Modern workplaces often function like imperial courts, with unwritten codes and performance expectations that can clash with biblical convictions. Corporate retreats may include activities or entertainment that conflict with Christian values, pressuring employees to choose between belonging and integrity. Performance metrics incentivize short-term gains, sometimes at the expense of ethical standards such as truthfulness in advertising or fairness in contracting. Like Daniel, believers in these contexts must master technical competencies while discerning when to refuse directives that undermine justice or exploit vulnerable populations. Open communication channels—formal ethics committees or anonymous reporting systems—can serve as modern equivalents of Daniel's conversation with the steward, offering structured opportunities to negotiate conscience-based requests. Whistleblowing may represent a last resort, akin to standing in the lion's den, but Daniel's example reminds us that integrity first requires disciplined relationships with decision-makers built on proven reliability. Employee resource groups or informal prayer circles form covenant communities that sustain faith under pressure, and mentoring relationships model vocational excellence grounded in servant leadership. Understanding corporate "renaming" occurs when organizational rebranding efforts co-opt personal mission statements, prompting believers to resist identity shifts that contradict their primary allegiance to Christ. By applying principles from Daniel's food test, modern professionals can propose limited trials—piloting ethical marketing approaches or flexible work arrangements—to demonstrate feasibility of faith-informed practices.

2.5.2 Exile in Academic Institutions

Universities represent today's Chaldean training programs, with curricula that reshape ideals through prescribed theories and research paradigms. Students face pressure to conform to dominant ideological trends—secular humanism, critical theory, or moral relativism—often embedded in course requirements and campus culture. Academic renaming occurs through adoption of jargon and identities aligned with institutional branding, risking displacement of theological vocabulary. Yet, as Daniel did, Christian scholars can excel in their disciplines, contributing peer-reviewed articles and conference presentations while filtering methods through biblical categories. Forming study cohorts and chaplaincy networks parallels exile prayer cells, providing spaces for collective lament and confessional critique of oppressive ideologies. Sabbatical practices, such as media fasts or restorative retreats, counter the 24/7 academic grind, echoing Sabbath disciplines. Negotiating syllabi boundaries—requesting alternative readings or assignments consistent with conscience—mirrors Daniel's diplomatic request for a diet trial. Professors who model intellectual humility, acknowledging gaps in secular frameworks and pointing to divine revelation, serve as modern interpreters of dreams, guiding peers toward truth that transcends academic paradigms.

2.5.3 Exile in Digital Spaces

Online platforms function as new Babylonian plazas where identities are constructed through avatars, usernames, and follower counts—modern equivalents of renaming. Algorithms collectivize preferences, shaping newsfeeds and cultural consumption in ways that mirror the imperial curriculum of the Chaldeans. Social media banquets tempt believers with viral challenges, influencer-sponsored products, and moral inversion, pressuring conformity to trending values. Yet believers can practice digital sabbaths, scheduling screen-free intervals and using content filters to resist algorithmic re-education. Online covenant communities—virtual small groups and prayer chats—create safe harbors for confession and encouragement, mitigating isolation. Thoughtful curation of digital diets—subscribing to gospel-centered channels, engaging with scriptural meditation apps—reflects Daniel's vegetable regimen, fostering spiritual health. Digital literacy involves recognizing the hidden curriculum in platform design and using privacy settings as contemporary equivalents of dietary boundaries. When cultural mandates clash with conscience—such as participation in deplatforming or cancel culture—believers can model restorative justice by promoting dialogue and refusing punitive echoes of the lion's-den mentality. In every virtual space, Daniel's blend of engagement, discernment, and disciplined witness offers a template for flourishing as exiles in the digital age.

2.6 Spiritual Habits That Anchor Identity

2.6.1 Daily Immersion in Scripture to Resist Narrative Capture

The practice of daily Scripture reading served as an anchor for Daniel's identity amid Babylon's competing narratives, reminding him that his primary allegiance lay with the living God rather than with shifting imperial ideologies. By setting aside deliberate time each day to engage the Torah, Daniel reenacted the covenantal rhythms of Israel, reinforcing truths about divine sovereignty and faithfulness long after the temple's fall. This commitment countered the Babylonian curriculum's subtle indoctrination, which taught its students to interpret history through omens and astrology instead of through God's redemptive purposes. As Daniel read and reflected, the promises of Jeremiah and the precedents of Moses and the psalmists resonated afresh, sustaining hope in seasons of cultural dissonance (Jeremiah 31:33). Regular Scripture engagement also sharpened Daniel's discernment, enabling him to distinguish between ethical absolutes and socially constructed norms. When confronted with royal decrees that mandated idolatrous worship, he could recall the commandment against bowing to other gods, strengthening his resolve (Exodus 20:3–5). The discipline of meditating on God's Word day and night as prescribed in Joshua 1:8 became a living practice for Daniel, aligning his affections and affording spiritual clarity when imperial policies threatened to blur moral boundaries. Through sustained immersion, he internalized the narrative arc that begins with creation, winds through exile, and climaxes in restoration—an arc that reframed his personal hardships as chapters in God's larger redemptive story. This habit also fostered a posture of humility, for the text revealed Daniel's own propensity to fear or self-reliance, prompting confession and renewed dependence (Psalm 119:11). In addition, consistent engagement with Scripture cultivated gratitude, as Daniel rehearsed God's past deliverances—such as the exodus from Egypt—and applied those lessons to his own captivity (Psalm 105:37–42). Over time, the words of the prophets and poets shaped his inner monologue, generating spontaneous prayers that echoed biblical language rather than Babylonian incantations. This internal library of truth equipped him to counsel kings with wisdom that transcended human insight, as when he interpreted Nebuchadnezzar's dream by invoking God's role as revealer of mysteries (Daniel 2:28). In contemporary terms, deliberate Scripture immersion functions as a form of cognitive inoculation against ideological saturation, protecting hearts and minds from adopting values that contradict the gospel. By structuring reading plans around thematic seasons—lament, praise, covenant promise—believers today can mirror Daniel's anchoring practice, using Scripture as both compass and lifeline. The habit of daily engagement thus prepares the way for other spiritual rhythms, notably fixed-hour prayer, which sustains dialogue with God in the midst of life's demands.

2.6.2 Fixed-Hour Prayer to Mark Time as Belonging to God

Daniel's unwavering commitment to praying three times a day illustrates how fixed-hour prayer can sanctify secular spaces and reclaim fragmented time for divine encounter (Daniel 6:10). In an environment that prized efficiency and unbroken loyalty to the state, Daniel's scheduled pauses demonstrated that every moment, even the busiest, ultimately belonged to the Ancient of Days. These regular prayer intervals interrupted Babylon's relentless pace, serving as sacred signposts that reoriented attention toward God's throne rather than toward human systems of power. Establishing set prayer times required both discipline and courage, for each public posture of kneeling by his window risked imperial censure. Yet Daniel's consistency taught observers that obedience to God's bidding eclipses fear of earthly consequences, shaping a witness that transcended mere words. The Psalms provided content for these prayers—confession, petition, and praise—ensuring that Daniel's intercession remained rooted in biblical language even when scribes and priests were absent (Psalm 55:17). His corporate posture in solitude foreshadows the church's later monastic hours while also demonstrating that prayer is not confined to designated worship venues. Each session of prayer rejuvenated Daniel's spirit, enabling him to face subsequent challenges with steady confidence rather than reactive anxiety. The discipline also educated his emotions, teaching his heart to trust God before crises struck, so that fear could never claim the first watch of the day. As his habit became visible to palace staff, it invited respect rather than scorn, for even pagan officials perceived that an unseen power sustained his composure under pressure (Daniel 6:16). When examined by Darius, Daniel could point to established practice rather than spontaneous rebellion, illustrating how fixed rhythms legitimize counter-cultural convictions. In our context, believers can adopt fixed-hour prayer using smartphone reminders or analog watches, embedding brief sanctuaries of conversation within workdays and family routines. Prayer anchors the soul in hope, reminding disciples that history unfolds under God's watchful eye, even when daily schedules suggest otherwise. This rhythm of dialogue naturally extends into communal lament and confession, equipping believers to share burdens and renew collective vision.

2.6.3 Practicing Hospitality and Generosity as Counter-Liturgies to Imperial Abundance

In a society that measured status by wealth and feasting, Daniel and his companions exemplified a counter-intuitive posture of generous hospitality that subverted Babylon's consumerist ethos. By sharing limited resources with fellow exiles—such as dividing portions of their acceptable food—they modeled covenant solidarity rather than individual preservation. Their generosity echoed Israel's jubilee principle of land and resource redistribution, reminding exiles that God's economy values equitable stewardship over competitive accumulation (Leviticus 25:10). When imperial banquets flaunted abundance to demonstrate divine favor, Daniel's table became a site of grace, where the invisible sovereign provided through simple fare. Hospitality in exile also extended to prayer and prayerful listening, as Daniel opened his home to fellow believers for joint study of Torah, nurturing a communal intimacy that transcended geographic dislocation. The prophetic tradition had linked justice for the poor with authentic worship (Isaiah 58:6–7); Daniel's generosity thus functioned as embodied theology, attesting that feeding the hungry outranks ritual sacrifice in God's assessment. In contexts where exiles depended on imperial charity, refusing texture-rich meals could have been met with disdain; yet Daniel's integrity in sharing scarce provisions testified to an alternative economy grounded in divine provision. Contemporary believers participate in similar counter-liturgies when they host neighbors of diverse backgrounds for modest meals, declaring through action that community transcends consumer status. Financial generosity toward the vulnerable—whether refugees, the unemployed, or orphans—stands as another rebellion against systems that hoard wealth for privileged insiders. Such practices reshape local cultures, forming networks of mutual care that witness to God's cyclical economy of blessing. In corporate or campus contexts, small acts of generosity—sharing resources, time, or expertise—challenge transactional mindsets that equate human worth with productivity. Daniel's hospitality extended beyond food; he used his influence to negotiate relief for exiled populations, foreshadowing modern advocacy work that aligns policy counsel with compassion. Generosity thus becomes a spiritual discipline, cultivating hearts that trust God's sufficiency rather than clutching resources out of fear. As this chapter transitions toward Daniel's deeper tests in royal courts and lion's dens, these spiritual habits remain the bedrock, ensuring that exile identity endures not as embittered survival but as vibrant witness to God's sustaining presence.

Conclusion

Daniel's early tests underscore a timeless principle: adversity can either erode fidelity or distill character. From the heartbreak of deportation to the subtleties of renaming and dietary compromise, each experience sharpened his vision of what constitutes true allegiance. These formative trials did more than preserve an ancient heritage; they inaugurated practices—Scripture immersion, structured prayer, covenantal hospitality—that anchored identity amid flux. The intertwining of personal discipline and communal solidarity equipped Daniel not only to withstand immediate pressures but also to interpret empires' deepest dreams and visions. His example challenges modern believers to face their own "Babylons" with strategic wisdom and unwavering courage, trusting that God's purposes endure beyond every displaced setting. As we move into the heart of Daniel's prophetic revelations and imperial encounters, the identity forged in these early tests will illuminate how steadfast faith navigates both courtly corridors and cosmic conflicts.

Chapter 3 – The Discipline of Devotion: Prayer and Wisdom under Pressure

In worlds shaped by shifting powers and relentless demands, devotion emerges as the wellspring of clarity and courage. Daniel's night of intercession amid a death decree reminds us that crises—whether imperial dreams or modern deadlines—are invitations to deeper dependence rather than occasions for frantic problem-solving alone. Prayer and meditation infuse the soul with horizon-stretching insight, enabling visionaries to decode hidden patterns and speak truth with both authority and humility. Yet devotion is more than escape; it is the crucible in which character and wisdom coalesce, equipping believers to engage every arena—from boardrooms to battlefields—with creativity and integrity. This chapter traces how disciplined rhythms of confession, petition, and praise undergird communal solidarity, fortify inner resilience, and order time amid competing loyalties. By learning from Daniel's steadfast example, readers discover practices that transform anxiety into expectancy, information overload into divine revelation, and isolated faith into vibrant communities of disciplined devotion.

3.0 Situating Devotion in an Age of Anxious Empires

Empires, whether ancient or modern, generate anxiety by magnifying human limitation and magnifying the reach of centralized power. Babylon's architecture, its ziggurats and processional ways, was designed to dwarf citizens physically and psychologically, reminding them that the state's authority towered over individual hopes. Today's globalized markets and always-on media streams accomplish something similar, placing people under deadlines and metrics that seem too vast to master. When deadlines loom, adrenaline spikes, and prayer can feel like a luxury rather than a necessity, yet Daniel's story insists that devotion is exactly what secures access to the wisdom that emergencies require. Prayer transforms crisis timelines by inserting eternity's perspective into the ticking clock, reframing the meaning of "delay" and "success" in light of the God who dwells outside time. Devotion also realigns loyalties, moving the heart's center of gravity from survival instinct to kingdom fidelity. In a culture where professional identity is often tethered to performance, cultivating daily liturgies of surrender gently pries fingers off the illusion that self-reliance safeguards the future. The act of bowing the knee when the empire demands frantic productivity becomes a prophetic declaration that the Most High alone governs both minutes and millennia. Scripture illustrates this rhythm repeatedly: Elijah withdraws to the brook of Kerith before confronting Ahab, and Jesus rises early to pray before feeding crowds and engaging critics (1 Kings 17:2-4; Mark 1:35-38). These patterns suggest that devotion is not escapism but the strategic pause that births Spirit-inspired solutions. Daniel's generation exemplifies such devotion under pressure, and their story primes us to see how prayerful dependence positions believers to interpret mysteries that paralyze powerful institutions. The unfolding narrative of the forgotten dream spotlights this dynamic, revealing how crisis becomes the canvas on which disciplined devotion paints divine insight.

3.1 The Crisis of the Forgotten Dream (Daniel 2)

3.1.1 Royal Panic and the Death Decree

Nebuchadnezzar's sleepless night exposes an empire's fragility, for a single unsettled monarch can upend the security of an entire bureaucracy. Babylon boasts libraries of omen texts, yet its most learned counselors freeze when asked to recall what the king has forgotten. Their protest that no human can perform such a feat inadvertently sets the stage for Yahweh, the revealer of mysteries, to display His supremacy. The edict to execute all wise men unravels the façade of Babylonian wisdom, showing that political power easily morphs into lethal threat when insecurity rules the throne. The swiftness of the decree underlines how institutions rooted in fear treat people as disposable assets, not bearers of divine image. Daniel, although relatively new to the court, is swept into the death list—a vivid reminder that righteous individuals do not receive immunity from collective crises. His calm inquiry of Arioch reflects both courage and wisdom; he gathers facts before reacting emotionally, modeling Proverbs' counsel that prudent understanding precedes decisive action (Proverbs 18:13). Nebuchadnezzar's demand for simultaneous revelation and interpretation also exposes every counterfeit epistemology that claims authority apart from divine disclosure. The moment highlights humanity's intrinsic longing for ultimate truth, even when it surfaces as tyrannical anxiety. Daniel's request for time, granted by a king unwilling to grant the same to lifelong advisers, demonstrates that favor often follows previous faithfulness and God-given composure. As political tension tightens, the narrative pivots toward the power of communal intercession, reinforcing that crises best drive believers into shared devotion rather than isolated despair.

3.1.2 Night-Long Intercession with Friends

Daniel's first response to existential threat is not strategy but prayer, and he refuses to pray alone. He gathers Hananiah, Mishael, and Azariah, proving that friendship forged in earlier trials blossoms into spiritual alliance when stakes escalate. Their united plea underscores that corporate intercession multiplies faith, echoing Jesus' later promise that where two or three agree, heaven responds (Matthew 18:19-20). The four friends likely prayed familiar psalms—perhaps Psalm 46, which celebrates God as refuge amid nations in uproar—infusing ancient words with immediate relevance. Throughout the night they wrestle, not to change God's disposition, but to align their hearts with His sovereign plan, embodying Paul's exhortation to present requests with thanksgiving so that peace surpasses understanding (Philippians 4:6-7). Darkness around them intensifies spiritual vigilance; every tick of the water clock reminds them that soldiers will soon patrol Babylon's streets to seize condemned sages. Yet petition is laced with hope because covenant memory fuels imagination; if God split seas and stilled suns, He can certainly recall a royal dream. Their prayers likely include confession of dependence, surrender of reputation, and plea for mercy upon the innocent, expanding concern beyond personal safety to include pagan colleagues. Shared vulnerability turns a rented room into sacred space, evidence that church can assemble wherever saints unite in need. When the mystery is unveiled in a vision, it arrives not to an isolated mystic but to the one who sought God in fellowship, illustrating that revelation is often entrusted to those who love community. This night of prayer prepares the friends for public proclamation, moving them from hidden supplication to courageous witness.

3.1.3 Revelation of the Mystery and Humble Reception

As dawn approaches, God discloses the dream and its meaning to Daniel, answering not only the what but also the why behind Nebuchadnezzar's turmoil. Daniel awakens to certainty that the Most High orchestrates history's succession of kingdoms, symbolized by gold, silver, bronze, iron, and clay. Instead of racing to announce his breakthrough, he first internalizes the gravity of grace, recognizing that such wisdom is a gift, not a personal achievement. The humility with which he receives the revelation contrasts sharply with the self-aggrandizing posture common in Babylon's diviners. Daniel's immediate impulse to worship shows that sacred knowledge is safe only in hearts bowed before its Giver. The content of the dream reframes geopolitical realities, revealing that Babylon's golden splendor is temporary and that an uncut stone—a kingdom not forged by human hands—will topple all empires. This interpretive lens comforts exiles and indicts arrogant rulers simultaneously, for it declares that sovereignty ultimately resides with God alone. Daniel's refusal to monetize or manipulate the revelation underscores devotion's purity; he neither seeks personal glory nor manipulates the information for political leverage. The vision's breadth confirms that prayer grants access to divine horizons, enabling believers to see both current crises and eschatological hope in a single gaze. This interior posture of humble clarity equips Daniel to step confidently into the throne room, bridging private devotion with public responsibility. The progression from revelation to response illustrates that wisdom's first assignment is stewardship, not display.

3.1.4 Hymn of Praise: Theology in Song

Before confronting the king, Daniel breaks into doxology, articulating a hymn that exalts God for changing times and seasons, removing kings and setting up kings (Daniel 2:20-23). This spontaneous worship crystallizes theology into melody, etching truth onto the memory of every listener across coming generations. Praise here functions as spiritual warfare, pushing back fear and sealing the revelation in gratitude rather than anxiety. The hymn affirms that wisdom and power belong to God, not to human intellect or imperial might, making worship the rightful response whenever heaven's mysteries intersect earth's need. By praising before deliverance is confirmed, Daniel models faith that rests in God's nature rather than in circumstantial outcomes. The emphasis on God's gift of wisdom to the lowly counters Babylonian meritocracy, elevating humility as the posture that attracts revelation. Singing theology also prepares Daniel's emotions for the court appearance; melody softens apprehension and aligns affections with truth. Corporate memory is forged in song, and later generations of exiles and early Christians alike would echo similar hymns under persecution, demonstrating music's power to sustain courage. Daniel's hymn transitions seamlessly from private gratitude to public proclamation, reminding us that personal devotion fuels public testimony. Having centered his heart, he proceeds to the palace carrying confidence rooted in worship, not self-confidence.

3.1.5 Audience with the King—Wisdom Coupled with Courage

Daniel enters Nebuchadnezzar's presence bearing both the dream and its interpretation, yet he begins by redirecting credit away from himself, declaring that no wise man could reveal the mystery but that there is a God in heaven who does (Daniel 2:27-28). This confession subverts the court's hierarchy by elevating a foreign deity above Babylon's pantheon in the very room dedicated to imperial supremacy. Speaking truth to power entails respecting the ruler's person while challenging the ruler's pride, and Daniel achieves this balance through courtesy paired with prophetic boldness. He recounts the dream exactly, validating divine authenticity before offering interpretation, thereby removing any suspicion of guesswork. When he pronounces that the king's kingdom will not last, Daniel demonstrates that genuine wisdom does not pander to authority but serves authority with truth. The courage to deliver a destabilizing message arises from the night of intercession, suggesting that prayer is training ground for prophetic speech. Nebuchadnezzar's eventual prostration before Daniel highlights how devotion can invert social structures, placing an exile above an emperor in the recognition of divine revelation. Daniel's request for promotion of his friends signals loyalty to community and underscores that individual favor should cascade into collective blessing. The scene closes with Babylon's ruler acknowledging Yahweh as "God of gods," a testimony wrung from crisis and sealed by disciplined devotion. This outcome prepares the narrative transition toward a fuller theology of prayerful dependence, showing how intercession, revelation, praise, and public witness form an integrated whole.

3.2 A Theology of Prayerful Dependence

3.2.1 Confession That Aligns the Heart

Prayer begins with confession because recognizing misplaced confidence detoxes the soul from self-reliance. Daniel's prayers in later chapters illustrate consistent acknowledgment of national and personal sin, reflecting the conviction that unconfessed guilt blocks relational intimacy with God (Daniel 9:4-6). Confession is not an exercise in shame but an act of recalibration, realigning desires with covenant truth. It deflates pride and opens space for divine wisdom to enter, for God opposes the proud but gives grace to the humble (James 4:6). The act names false loves—status, control, reputation—and lays them before the throne, liberating the heart from their covert tyranny. Confession also deepens empathy; by acknowledging his own failings, the pray-er grows patient with others' weaknesses, cultivating a gracious community. In corporate settings, shared confession dismantles illusions of spiritual hierarchy, reminding assembled believers that all stand on equal ground at the foot of the cross. The spiritual practice trains discernment, helping identify habitual patterns that sabotage devotion, such as resentment or chronic hurry. It opens eyes to systemic sin as well as personal transgression, broadening intercession to societal repentance. By beginning prayer with confession, the soul is primed to petition without presumption, ready to receive and steward divine gifts. This realigned posture leads naturally into asking, for hearts emptied of pretense are now free to seek bold kingdom breakthroughs.

3.2.2 Petition for Kingdom Breakthrough

Petition moves beyond maintenance prayers toward bold requests that God's sovereignty manifest in tangible circumstances. Daniel's plea for the dream's revelation involves high stakes, for countless lives hinge upon divine intervention. Petition recognizes God as the ultimate source of solutions and invites His power to bear upon seemingly intractable situations. Jesus' model prayer, urging disciples to ask for daily bread and kingdom come, demonstrates that big and small needs alike matter in the economy of grace (Matthew 6:9-13). Effective petition is rooted in scriptural promise, appealing to God's character rather than manipulating outcomes. It refuses fatalism, asserting that history bends toward divine purposes but that human intercession mysteriously participates in that bending. Petition trains perseverance, as repeated requests cultivate both patience and expectancy, forging steel in the soul. Such prayers enlarge imagination, inspiring creative ideas that align with heaven's agenda; sometimes the answer arrives as courage to act, other times as circumstances shift dramatically. Petition keeps disciples engaged in the tension between "already" and "not yet," interceding for healing, justice, and revival even when partial fulfillment seems discouragingly slow. As God responds, gratitude flows, cycling naturally into the doxology of praise.

3.2.3 Praise That Reorients Perspective

Praise functions as a corrective lens, shifting focus from looming threats to the incomparable greatness of God. Daniel's hymn models how worship metabolizes anxiety into adoration, reminding the soul that the One who moves constellations also oversees court intrigues. Praise is not denial of difficulty; it is robust acknowledgment that God's resources eclipse the crisis's demand. In practice, praising through song, spoken word, or silent meditation infuses emotional resilience, raising spiritual temperature above fear's frigid grip. The Psalms consistently marry pain and praise, demonstrating that lament can culminate in confident worship (Psalm 42:11). Declaring God's attributes—faithfulness, mercy, omnipotence—builds theological muscle memory that activates under duress. When believers exalt God publicly, they invite onlookers into an alternative narrative where hope is rational and despair irrational. Praise also breaks chains of self-centeredness, redirecting attention outward and upward. Neurological studies indicate that gratitude rewires the brain toward optimism; biblically grounded praise accomplishes this at a deeper spiritual level. Sustained adoration generates overflow into generosity and service, for beholding divine beauty births desire to reflect it. As perspective elevates, prayers expand, birthing intercession not merely for personal deliverance but for systemic transformation, linking seamlessly to corporate solidarity.

3.2.4 Corporate Intercession and Covenantal Solidarity

While private prayer cultivates intimacy, corporate intercession forges unity and amplifies spiritual authority. The four Hebrews' night vigil illustrates how collective petitions release answers with communal impact. In Acts, the church prays Peter out of prison, proving that united cry shakes prison doors (Acts 12:5-17). Corporate prayer creates synergies of faith; one believer's testimony stokes another's hope, forming a feedback loop of expectation. It democratizes ministry, ensuring that breakthroughs are attributed to God's people rather than charismatic individuals. Gathering intergenerationally transmits spiritual DNA, teaching younger believers to shoulder responsibility for kingdom outcomes. Corporate rhythms—fasts, vigils, responsive readings—also construct spiritual culture, shaping organizational identity around dependence rather than strategy. In hostile contexts, group prayer emboldens witness, converting fear into collective courage. This solidarity embarks on mutual submission, each participant deferring to discerned consensus, reducing the risk of lone-wolf missteps. When corporate petitions align with God's heart, He often orchestrates coincidences—providential meetings, financial provision—that surpass any plan. Such experiences cultivate holy expectancy, compelling communities to pray the future into the present.

3.2.5 Praying the Future into the Present

Prophetic intercession stands on eschatological promises, pulling tomorrow's certainties into today's uncertainties. Daniel's prayers later engage seventy-week timelines, demonstrating that apocalyptic hope informs present obedience. New-Testament believers echo this by praying "Maranatha," yearning for Christ's return while laboring in mission (Revelation 22:20). Praying future realities transforms character, producing perseverance emboldened by assured victory. It reframes suffering, recognizing it as birth pangs of a kingdom that cannot be shaken (Romans 8:18-25; Hebrews 12:28). Such prayer fosters strategic imagination, prompting initiatives—church planting, justice advocacy—that anticipate the age to come. Hope-saturated intercession guards against cynicism when earthly systems disappoint, reinforcing that ultimate justice is appointed by God, not merely legislated by human courts. It also tempers triumphalism, for longing for consummation acknowledges that fullness is pending, cultivating humility. Praying eschatologically integrates lament and joy, for the one who anticipates resurrection can grieve loss without despair. This future-oriented dependency propels devotion into daily routines, spacing corridors of time with expectancy. As believers step into boardrooms, classrooms, or neighborhoods, they carry particular awareness that every decision echoes in eternity. This forward-leaning posture prepares the heart for discerning God's whispers amid noisy environments, a transition we will explore in the next segment on practical devotion within high-performance cultures.

3.3 Practising Devotion in High-Performance Cultures

3.3.1 Crafting a Rule of Life for Busy People A Rule of Life provides a scaffold for devotion that integrates seamlessly into packed schedules, ensuring that spiritual rhythms are not casualties of frenetic work days. Practitioners begin by mapping out fixed commitments—family meals, worship gatherings, and rest periods—then insert prayer and Scripture slots around these immovable anchors. The process starts with a realistic assessment of available time, acknowledging that perfectionist zeal often leads to abandonment rather than sustainability. Establishing micro-rhythms—five-minute breath prayers between meetings or Scripture readings during coffee breaks—guards against the illusion that only lengthy sessions count as "real" devotion. The Rule also designates seasons for deeper engagement, such as quarterly retreats or weekly extended sabbaths, echoing Jesus' practice of withdrawing regularly for communion with the Father (Mark 1:35). Accountability partners review the Rule periodically, celebrating fidelity and renegotiating commitments as life circumstances change, preventing legalism and fostering grace. Incorporating margin—buffer zones between appointments—creates breathing space where spontaneous prayer or acts of compassion can unfold without guilt. A written Rule externalizes intention, making spiritual aspirations concrete and measurable, much like athletic training plans track progress toward endurance goals. Over time, habituated rhythms shift from effortful disciplines to natural expressions of identity, so that devotion ceases to feel like an obligation and becomes as instinctive as checking email. The Rule's flexibility allows for integration of liturgical seasons—Advent, Lent, Pentecost—infusing ordinary rhythms with communal celebration. Digital tools support the process by sending reminders for prayer intervals or turning off distractions during designated "inner room" times (Matthew 6:6). Journaling reflections on adherence to the Rule deepen self-awareness, surfacing hidden idols—achievement, acclaim, control—that vie for misplaced devotion. Revisiting the Rule on retreats enables recalibration: pruning practices that no longer serve spiritual growth and planting new ones that reflect emerging needs. This dynamic covenant with oneself and God aligns time management with kingdom priorities, preventing high-performance cultures from dictating devotion's tempo. Transitioning from personal Rule-making, we turn to strategies for protecting the inner room from digital encroachment.

3.3.2 Digital Boundaries That Guard the Inner Room In an era when smartphones buzz persistently, guarding the "inner room" of the soul demands intentional digital boundaries. Unchecked notifications fragment attention, eroding capacity for sustained prayer and deep reading of Scripture. Practitioners start by auditing app usage—identifying time-sinks such as social media or news feeds—and uninstalling or restricting those that undermine focus. Enabling "Do Not Disturb" during prayer blocks intrusive pings, converting physical isolation into digital solitude. Prayer apps, when used judiciously, can supply liturgical prompts without distracting gamified features that hijack attention. Email and messaging are configured to batch-deliver at set intervals, so that devotees engage technology on their terms rather than responding to every stimulus reflexively. Families establish communal tech-free zones during meals or evening hours, reinforcing that relationships transcend digital connectivity. Digital sabbaths—entire days off screens—recalibrate affections away from virtual affirmation toward embodied presence with loved ones and God's creation. Habits of scrolling upon waking are replaced by reaching for a journal or Bible, setting an intentional tone for the day. Device fasts around bedtime improve sleep quality and create space for meditative prayer, reflecting Psalm 4:4's injunction to "be still and know that I am God." These rhythms echo Daniel's pattern of withdrawal for prayer, adapted to twenty-first-century temptations. Regular "technology fasts" challenge believers to confront underlying anxieties—fear of missing out or need for approval—by enduring brief digital silence. Virtual accountability groups share boundary practices and encourage one another in maintaining guardrails. Training in digital literacy helps discern algorithmic persuasion, preventing subconscious re-education by corporate interests. Intentional use of technology transforms tools into servants rather than masters, preserving the inner room as a sanctuary for unhurried devotion. Having secured digital frontiers, we next explore how embodied habits reinforce prayerful presence.

3.3.3 Embodied Habits: Breath Prayer, Posture, and Place

Devotion engages mind, heart, and body, and simple embodied practices root prayer in the physical self. Breath prayer—synchronizing inhalation and exhalation with short petitions such as "Lord, have mercy" or "Come, Holy Spirit"—anchors attention when thoughts drift. This rhythmic pattern parallels Daniel's steady petition even under threat, reminding modern disciples that bodily cues can sustain mental focus. Posture influences mindset: kneeling conveys humility, standing evokes readiness, and lying prostrate expresses total surrender, each posture inviting meditation on corresponding biblical themes (Psalm 95:6). Designating a physical prayer corner—complete with a chair, cushion, or icon—signals the body that entering this space means shifting into sacred time. Scents like frankincense or hymnal art can trigger associative memory, deepening immersion. Walking prayer—stylite tradition in new form—uses rhythmic footsteps to internalize Scripture, turning movement into a form of lectio divina (Genesis 3:8's image of God walking in the garden). Incorporating gestures such as laying hands on one's heart during confession or raising hands in praise engages kinesthetic learners. Seasonal rotation of devotional artifacts—Advent wreaths, Lenten crosses, Pentecost doves—refreshes attention. These embodied cues circumvent mind-only approaches that falter under stress, offering multisensory anchors to divine presence. They imbue daily chores—washing dishes, folding laundry—with contemplative potential, as each action becomes an invitation to "pray without ceasing" (1 Thessalonians 5:17). Over time, the body's memory internalizes devotion, so that worship arises spontaneously even amid busy routines. With embodied habits established, practitioners gain resilience for rapid decision-making, the focus of the next section.

3.3.4 Wisdom Frameworks for Rapid Decision-Making High-pressure cultures demand swift choices, yet knee-jerk reactions often betray values or ethical commitments. Wisdom frameworks—structured questions drawn from biblical principles—equip believers to vet decisions in real time. Simple filters ask: Does this honor God as Lord? Does it serve neighbor's good? Does it align with Scripture's clear commands? This triad echoes Jesus' summary of the law and prophets (Matthew 22:37-40). Under deadline, mental checklists help bypass emotional reactivity, channeling conscience toward kingdom outcomes. When choices involve complex trade-offs, practitioners pause for micro-examinations of conscience, naming underlying fears—loss of status, approval, security—that may distort judgment. Consulting trusted mentors or accountability circles by quick messaging ensures that decisions gain collective wisdom rather than private impulses. Biblical case studies—Daniel's refusal of royal foods, Nehemiah's rebuild decisions—serve as mental precedents, supplying analogies for modern dilemmas. Breath prayer precedes choice, slowing heart rate enough for those frameworks to activate neural pathways associated with reflective thought. Post-decision, reflective debriefing assesses outcomes against ethical standards, reinforcing learning for future scenarios. Over time, repeated use of wisdom frameworks creates a moral muscle memory that transforms rapid decisions into faithful responses. This process bridges devotion with discernment, enabling application of revealed insight under pressure. Equipped with such frameworks, believers cultivate resilience—our next focus—prepared to withstand the stresses of demanding environments.

3.3.5 Resilience Under Pressure True resilience emerges not from stoic force of will but from rhythms that oscillate between action and restoration. Devotional practices cushion high-intensity engagement with restorative counters: lament sessions acknowledge strain, confession releases shame, and praise rebuilds hope. Neuroscience shows that emotional resilience correlates with regulated stress responses, and spiritual disciplines function as practical tools for such regulation (Philippians 4:6-7). Incorporating brief pauses—stretch breaks, silent centering—resets physiology, preventing chronic activation of fight-or-flight pathways. Community rituals, such as midweek prayer gatherings, inject collective encouragement into weary weeks. Storytelling about divine faithfulness in past crises offers cognitive reappraisal, reframing setbacks as opportunities for grace. Periodic solitary retreats—mirroring Daniel's withdrawal for prayer—renew perspective away from performance metrics. Journaling both successes and failures in spiritual disciplines fosters self-compassion and adaptive learning. Celebrating small victories—a day kept according to the Rule, a well-chosen decision under duress—affirms progress and sustains motivation. Physical exercise, rest, and appropriate nutrition amplify the body's capacity to endure, underscoring that stewardship of creation extends to self-care (1 Corinthians 6:19-20). Over time, resilience becomes not merely recovery from crisis but a capacity to thrive amid ongoing challenges. With resilience anchored, communities can advance from disciplined individuals to collaborative networks of devotion.

3.4 Discernment and Revelation—Translating Insight into Action

3.4.1 From Dreams to Data: Hearing God in a Noise-Saturated World In Babylon, dreams functioned as coded communications from gods, yet Daniel knew only Yahweh reliably revealed mysteries. Today's noise-saturated environments—information overload, social media chatter, constant news cycles—drown out divine promptings unless believers cultivate discernment. The first step is filtering inputs: curating trusted scripture-based resources and limiting time on speculative or sensationalist media. Just as Daniel waited for God to reveal the dream before interpreting it, modern disciples pause for reflective prayer before analyzing data sets or making projections. Decision-makers may hold "listening labs"—quiet sessions devoted to spiritual discernment rather than brainstorming—to identify values beyond raw metrics. Practices like "divine data walks"—noting patterns in nature or community that mirror scriptural truths—train the eyes to see God's fingerprints in everyday contexts. Regular fasting from digital noise creates receptive spaces for intuition, akin to the prophetic tradition of hearing God in the whisper rather than the storm (1 Kings 19:11-13). Teams can use contemplative pauses in meetings—moments of silence to sense God's guidance—preventing groupthink and opening the way for fresh insights. Over time, integrating prayer before data analysis yields patterns that align with kingdom priorities rather than merely organizational goals. Discernment becomes a corporate asset, guiding strategy in ways that exceed conventional problem-solving models. Transitioning from identifying divine signals to generating creative solutions brings us to the next subsection.

3.4.2 Spirit-Inspired Creativity for Complex Problems Complex challenges often defy linear solutions, requiring creative leaps that emerge only in the liminal spaces of devotion. The Spirit, described as the Giver of wisdom and insight (Isaiah 11:2), inspires ideas that transcend reductive frameworks. Historical examples include the early missionaries adapting ship travel to spread the gospel or Dietrich Bonhoeffer drafting reverse-disaster relief plans from prison. In corporate or nonprofit contexts, ideation sessions grounded in prayer can produce innovations that respect human dignity and environmental limits. Techniques like "holy huddles," where teams alternate silent reflection and brief sharing, foster a balance between inward listening and outward brainstorming. Scripture's diverse literary genres—poetry, narrative, prophecy—model multifaceted thinking that values metaphor and paradox, encouraging solution-finders to resist pure data-driven approaches. Recording ideas in prayer journals preserves embryonic insights that can mature over time, mirroring Daniel's preserved visions until the appointed hour (Daniel 8:26). Spirit-led creativity often emerges when teams step away from problem pressure into shared worship, resetting cognitive pathways. This creative flow empowers believers to tackle issues—climate change, systemic injustice, digital ethics—using imagination fertilized by God's kingdom vision. As novel solutions arise, ethical courage is required to bring them into public arenas, which we examine next.

3.4.3 Ethical Courage to Deliver Hard Truths with Hope

Receiving divine insight imposes responsibility to speak truth, even when it challenges powerful stakeholders. Daniel's interpretation of the writing on the wall (Daniel 5) confronted Belshazzar's sacrilege with uncompromising clarity. Such prophetic courage stems from conviction that God's assessment transcends human prestige, and that exposing injustice opens the way for genuine restoration. Modern leaders face parallel moments—identifying corporate malpractice, systemic bias, or destructive policies—and must deliver critiques infused with hope rather than merely condemnation. Courageous truth-telling involves framing feedback within a future-oriented vision, reassuring audiences that change leads to flourishing rather than punishment alone. Structures like "feedback covenants," where participants agree to receive correction with grace, create safe environments for hard conversations. Public apologies and restitution plans demonstrate that speaking truth is not an end but the start of redemptive processes. Ethical courage draws on devotional reservoirs—regular prayer, scriptural promises, community support—to withstand personal cost. Over time, such prophetic witness cultivates cultures where integrity and compassion co-exist, modeling kingdom life in the world. Having equipped individuals and teams for discerning, creative, and courageous action, the chapter now turns to building communities that sustain these patterns.

3.5 Cultivating Communities of Disciplined Devotion

3.5.1 Prayer Triads and Accountability Circles Small group structures like prayer triads—three-person partnerships—offer both privacy and mutual challenge, balancing confidentiality with diverse perspectives. Triads meet regularly, sharing personal needs, confessing struggles, and interceding with specificity, strengthening bonds and deepening vulnerability. Accountability circles expand this model to four to six members, allowing for broader feedback while preserving trust. These circles establish norms—confidentiality agreements, regular attendance, and shared commitments to Scripture and prayer—that guard against superficiality. Members rotate facilitation roles, ensuring that leadership skills develop across the group rather than concentrating in one individual. Structured agendas combine check-in questions, devotional readings, and intentional prayer segments, preventing time drift and maximizing depth. Tools like shared digital journals capture prayer requests and answered prayers, creating a collective memory of faithfulness. Circles practice "redemptive listening," where each voice is honored and interruptions are minimized, fostering empathy and theological reflection. Periodic retreats reconnect members beyond screen constraints, renewing relational capital. Triads and circles also serve as incubators for leadership development, preparing participants to launch similar groups and multiply communities of devotion. This networked approach ensures that disciplined practices outlast any single group, embedding them within broader ecclesial structures.

3.5.2 Liturgical Innovation for Offices, Classrooms, and Zoom Rooms

In diverse contexts—corporate offices, university classrooms, virtual meeting platforms—creative liturgies embed devotion into communal life. Morning stand-up meetings might begin with a one-minute silence or a shared Scripture reflection, modeling communal centering before task lists dominate. Professors open lectures with brief prayers for wisdom and love, signaling that all knowledge pursuit is undergirded by divine illumination. Virtual gatherings on Zoom integrate spiritual rhythms through screen-shared prayers, responsive liturgical slides, or breakout-room discussions of Scripture passages. Worship leaders can design bite-sized liturgies—two-line call-and-response prayers, one-verse meditations—that require minimal training yet yield maximal participation. Seasonal liturgical elements—Advent readings, Lenten reflections—rotate across academic semesters and fiscal quarters, weaving faith's narrative into organizational calendars. Recognizing diverse faith backgrounds, these innovations invite reflection rather than impose formulas, asking participants to consider universal longings such as justice, mercy, and hope. Feedback loops collect participant input, refining liturgies to remain resonant and culturally relevant. Such practices transform routine gatherings into sanctuaries of shared devotion, fostering unity amid diversity and granting sacred shape to otherwise transactional interactions. As these liturgies proliferate, they stitch together fragmentary contexts into a tapestry of disciplined communal worship.

3.5.3 Mentoring the Next Generation in Devotional Practice

Intentional mentorship transmits devotional traditions from experienced practitioners to emerging leaders, preventing loss of formative practices amid generational shifts. Mentors invite mentees into their own rhythms—inviting attendance at personal retreats, sharing prayer journals, and modeling Rule-of-Life adjustments. Rather than prescribing rigid formulas, mentors emphasize experimental learning: suggesting practices, reflecting together on outcomes, and iterating based on effectiveness. Mentoring relationships often feature shadowing opportunities—joining in prayer triads, observing liturgical innovations in action, and participating in ethical decision-making discussions. Reciprocal learning recognizes that younger generations contribute fresh perspectives on technology, culture, and global issues, enriching devotional practices for all involved. Mentors encourage mentees to develop their own Rule of Life, offering accountability and celebrating milestones. Establishing intergenerational cohorts—pairing pairs across age groups—creates mutual encouragement and prevents isolation. Formalized mentoring programs within churches, workplaces, and seminaries institutionalize this transfer, ensuring that devotional wisdom remains dynamic rather than fossilized. Through sustained relational investment, the next generation inherits not only techniques but the underlying vision of walking in disciplined dependence on God, ready to steward faith under pressure in their own eras and contexts.

3.6 Devotion Turned Public Service

3.6.1 Sustained Prayer as Preparation for Stewarding Influence

Sustained prayer furnishes the spiritual infrastructure required for leadership, forging roots of humility beneath branches of authority. Early morning petitions steady the heart before the day's negotiations begin, ensuring that convictions arise from communion rather than impulse. Daniel's pattern of worship, uninterrupted even by royal edicts, became the hidden storehouse from which he drew courage when addressing monarchs. Consistent intercession cultivates a sensitivity to God's voice, enabling leaders to perceive undercurrents—a king's unspoken anxieties or a nation's moral drift—that statistics alone cannot reveal. Prayerful dependence reorients decision-making from personal ambition to kingdom priorities, transforming policy proposals into acts of worship. As leaders petition God for wisdom, they demonstrate vulnerability that invites counsel and diffuses defensiveness among colleagues. The discipline teaches endurance, preventing exhaustion when challenges extend beyond any individual's capacity. When Daniel rose to interpret dreams or draft decrees, his words resonated with integrity because they emerged from time spent before the throne rather than from raw intellect. Sustained prayer also builds a reservoir of peace, so that crises do not trigger panic but spark immediate return to the inner room for refreshment. Leaders nurtured by prayer avoid the common trap of equating busyness with effectiveness, recognizing that strategic pauses often yield greater clarity than constant motion. Regular confession, woven into daily devotions, keeps power from inflating the ego, reminding leaders that every accolade derives from divine gifting. This humility undergirds credibility, so that when decision-makers enact reforms or challenge injustices, their voices carry weight beyond institutional rank. Moreover, communal intercession secures broader support, as teams who have prayed together cultivate mutual trust and shared vision. Shared prayer experiences become corporate memory, leaving an imprint on organizational culture that values spiritual discernment alongside technical skill. In this way, sustained prayer functions not as a private piety but as the corporate altar upon which all future leadership initiatives are consecrated. As devotion dresses the soul in garments of grace, it prepares believers to step into public spheres with wisdom and courage, setting the stage for the next chapter's focus on Daniel's rise as a policy adviser.

3.6.2 Foreshadowing Daniel's Rise as Chief of the Wise Men and Policy Adviser

Daniel's trajectory from exiled youth to chief counselor illustrates how devotion yields tangible platforms for kingdom influence. His reputation for divinely granted insight spread quickly through the palace corridors, prompting kings to value his judgments in matters of statecraft. Before receiving honors, Daniel first invested hours in prayer, petitioning God for clarity on both dreams and governance issues. His ability to interpret Nebuchadnezzar's vision authenticated his counsel, but it was sustained devotion that built the relational capital necessary for repeated audiences with the throne.

Leaders who emerge from humble devotion rather than self-promotion gain credibility that survives regime changes. When Belshazzar faced the writing on the wall, it was Daniel's consistent track record of faithfulness that prompted his summons amid political turmoil. His policies, shaped by prayerful reflection on God's justice and mercy, contributed to administrative reforms such as equitable tax collection and protection of minority rights under Darius. These public achievements did not eclipse his devotional life but grew out of it, illustrating that outward success must be rooted in inward communion. Daniel's example invites modern believers to view vocational advancement not as self-elevation but as an invitation to broaden gospel witness. As a policy adviser, he balanced obedience to earthly rulers with unwavering loyalty to Yahweh, modeling a dual-citizen posture that prophetically challenged imperial overreach. His rise served the common good—rescuing innocent lives, stabilizing economies, and promoting ethical governance—demonstrating that devotion-informed leadership benefits entire societies. By foreshadowing Daniel's ascent, we glimpse how prayer translates into strategic influence, encouraging readers to envision how their own vocational spheres might become platforms for kingdom values. This anticipation naturally leads into an exploration of how integrity in corridors of power emerges from a foundation of disciplined devotion.

3.6.3 Devotion as the Launchpad for Integrity in the Corridors of Power

The inner fire kindled by devotional disciplines radiates outward, igniting integrity in every professional interaction. Daniel's refusal to compromise on dietary practices translated into unassailable credibility when negotiating treaties, for colleagues recognized that his positions stemmed from principled devotion rather than political expediency. Integrity flourishes when decisions are rooted in unbroken communion with God, preventing rationalizations that adapt ethics to convenience. Devotion disciplines the conscience, sharpening awareness of ethical blind spots that often emerge under the pressures of advancement. In policy discussions, a leader formed by devotional rhythms resists lobbying tactics and special-interest entanglements, preferring transparent processes that reflect God's justice. The consistency of private practices—prayer at dawn, Scripture at midday—anchors public integrity, ensuring that power does not corrupt but is stewarded faithfully. Daniel's example shows that integrity is not mere adherence to codes but the embodiment of character shaped by God's presence. When political rivals or corporate competitors observed his fairness and compassion, they could attest that his faith was not a veneer but the source of his moral compass. Devotional communities provide accountability that reinforces such integrity, as peers who share prayer rhythms also challenge deviations from biblical standards. The synergy of private devotion and public ethics fosters trust within organizations, which in turn enhances effectiveness and social impact. Leaders thus trained become beacons, inspiring systemic change where governance or corporate cultures have drifted into self-interest. Viewed through this lens, devotion is less an escape from the world and more the propulsion system that drives authentic service within it. As we transition to Chapter 4, this launchpad of integrity sets the groundwork for examining how Daniel's devotion catalyzed his remarkable public ministry among the world's most powerful leaders.

Conclusion

The discipline of devotion reshapes both heart and context, knitting private prayer to public influence in a seamless garment of faithfulness. When crises threaten to unravel our confidence, the rhythms of Scripture, fixed-hour intercession, and communal lament reanchor us in the sovereign purposes of God. These spiritual habits carve channels through which divine wisdom flows into complex situations, making space for creative solutions and courageous truth-telling. As we move from the inner room to the corridors of power, the same devotional framework that bore Daniel through sleepless nights and imperial audiences continues to guide disciples today. Anchored in prayerful dependence, we are poised not merely to survive pressure but to steward influence for the flourishing of our communities and the glory of the One who reigns forever.

Chapter 4 – Serving with Integrity: Daniel the Statesman and Interpreter

When a foreign exile ascended to the highest councils of Babylon, his path did not follow that of self-advancement but that of a servant molded by devotion. Daniel's journey from captive youth to chief counselor illustrates how unwavering integrity, grounded in prayer and Scripture, equips a person to influence empires without surrendering conscience. His public service demonstrates that political savvy and spiritual fidelity need not conflict; instead, they can combine to produce governance characterized by justice, wisdom, and compassion. In a world where power frequently corrupts character, Daniel modeled an alternative: power exercised as sacred stewardship, guided by divine revelation rather than mere pragmatism. His ability to interpret dreams, shape policies, and mediate crises emerged from rhythms of private intercession and communal solidarity, forging a statesman for whom every administrative decision was an act of worship.

4.0 From Exile to Cabinet—Spiritual Foundations for Public Service

4.0.1 Exile Credentials: Why Displacement Often Forges the Best Civil Servants

Experiencing exile strips individuals of familiar safety nets, forcing reliance on inner resources and convictions that survive institutional collapse. Daniel and his friends were carried far from home without status or secure future, yet their displacement became the crucible that honed adaptability, cultural literacy, and empathy for other uprooted peoples. In Babylon, they learned to navigate unfamiliar protocols while retaining a distinct moral compass, a combination that civil administrations prize in crisis-management roles. Modern parallels appear in refugee professionals who, after forced migration, develop cross-cultural negotiation skills and a passion for justice that translate into effective public service. Exile tests character faster than comfort, exposing hidden anxieties and revealing whether values hold when convenience evaporates. Daniel's capacity to serve Nebuchadnezzar and later Darius with wisdom and loyalty—despite being labeled a foreigner—demonstrates how displacement can yield unparalleled credibility among diverse constituencies. His lived experience of loss informed policies that valued minority rights and fair treatment of captives, reflecting personal memory of hardship. Contemporary governments often recruit diaspora experts for infrastructure rebuilding and reconciliation processes precisely because their trials have shaped resilience and global vision. Exile credentials, rooted in survival rather than privilege, confer authenticity that helps leaders bridge tribal divisions and foster social cohesion. When institutions recognize these strengths, they benefit from officials whose character emerges from adversity rather than entitlement. This paradigm challenges prevailing assumptions that pedigree alone ensures leadership quality, instead affirming that tests of faith often repay institutions with innovative problem-solving and compassionate governance. As Daniel's example shows, displacement need not diminish influence but can amplify it, equipping exiles to advise kings and nations from a foundation of lived dependence on divine provision.

4.0.2 Statesmanship as a Divine Calling, Not a Secular Sidetrack

Statesmanship in Daniel's world was more than political maneuvering; it functioned as stewardship of social order under divine oversight. When Daniel accepted his role as counselor to Babylon's monarchs, he did not view public office as a departure from spiritual priorities but as a sacred arena for manifesting God's justice and mercy. His advice to kings transcended realpolitik, drawing on visions that portrayed God's sovereignty over human empires (Daniel 2:21). In aligning administrative counsel with theological conviction, Daniel reframed governance as participation in divine purpose rather than mere career advancement. This theological vision counters the modern tendency to bifurcate faith and work, treating spiritual commitments as weekend extras separate from weekday duties. Recognizing statesmanship as a divine calling empowers public servants to see their daily tasks—budget drafts, policy debates, legislative negotiations—as liturgical acts offered before the throne of heaven (Colossians 3:23). This perspective invites prayerful discernment at every stage of decision-making, acknowledging that moral clarity emerges not from polling data but from communion with the One who "removes kings and sets up kings" (Daniel 2:21). When offices become sanctuaries for justice, leaders echo biblical prophets who confronted kings from within courts, calling rulers to righteousness and warning them of covenantal consequences (1 Samuel 12; Isaiah 6). Such prophetic statesmanship carries risk but also the potential for transformational impact, as seen when Nebuchadnezzar issued edicts honoring Yahweh in response to Daniel's counsel. Viewing public service as divine vocation elevates the stakes of policy debates, reframes successes as participations in God's kingdom, and dignifies professional excellence as an act of worship. This integrated framework lays the groundwork for the prayer-policy pipeline through which devotion births wisdom for governance.

4.0.3 The Prayer-Policy Pipeline: How Communion with God Births Public Wisdom

Daniel's ascendancy to chief counselor was rooted in patterns of disciplined devotion that preceded every public engagement. Before tackling complex bureaucratic challenges or interpreting royal dreams, he first sought divine insight in prayer, modeling the "prayer-policy pipeline" by which spiritual communion fuels strategic acumen. This approach contrasts sharply with technocratic models that treat policymaking as the product of human analysis alone. Daniel's nighttime intercessions with Hananiah, Mishael, and Azariah paved the way for daybreak revelations that reshaped empire-wide decisions (Daniel 2:16–19). His habit of translating political quandaries into prayer themes underscores the principle that no policy should proceed without seeking God's mind (James 1:5). Embedded in this pipeline are regular reflection rhythms—Scripture meditation on justice passages, corporate confession of institutional sin, petition for communal flourishing, and doxology for anticipated breakthroughs. These spiritual inputs function like quality-control checkpoints, aligning policy proposals with biblical imperatives for mercy, equity, and stewardship. When Daniel drafted regulations on tax or trade, he did so from a posture of intercession for the welfare of exiles and natives alike, ensuring that governance served the common good rather than narrow interests. Modern civil servants who adopt this pipeline find that prayer reframes technical dilemmas within moral horizons, prompting solutions that balance economic viability with human dignity. Churches and training institutes can equip future policymakers with this integrated model, cultivating cohorts that move seamlessly from prayer rooms to planning sessions. By tracing Daniel's example, leaders learn that prophetic counsel requires both spiritual receptivity and strategic follow-through, enabling public service that resonates with eternal purpose.

4.0.4 Spiritual Authority vs. Positional Authority—Learning to Wield Both with Humility

Daniel's influence derived from a convergence of positional authority as chief of the wise men and spiritual authority as a conduit of heavenly revelation. While his office granted him entrée into royal councils, it was his reputation for divine insight that commanded enduring respect, even from pagan rulers. Distinguishing spiritual authority from positional power required humility, for spiritual authority rests on God's gifting rather than human appointment. Daniel demonstrated this when he credited God, not himself, for every interpretation, modeling servant-leadership that deflected personal aggrandizement (Daniel 2:28–30). This posture prevented the corrupting influence of power, ensuring that positions became platforms for divine purpose rather than stages for self-promotion. In modern settings, professionals may hold titles that confer decision-making power, yet their lasting impact depends on congruence between authority and authentic character. Spiritual authority manifests when leaders speak truth to power in sacrificial love, as Daniel did when confronting Belshazzar's sacrilege with uncompromising candor (Daniel 5). Positional authority, while potentially volatile, serves as a temporary vessel for implementing godly principles. Wielded with humility, positional power can enact policies that institutionalize justice and compassion; wielded without spiritual authority, it devolves into coercion and self-interest. The art of integrating both forms of authority calls for spiritual disciplines—regular confession to weaken pride, communal accountability to temper isolation, and retreat rhythms to recover perspective. As Daniel's career shows, leaders who practice this integration avoid the two pitfalls of despotic autonomy and powerless piety. They become bridges between divine wisdom and human governance, translating transcendent truths into tangible reforms. Understanding this interplay prepares public servants to serve with integrity, a theme we now see embodied in Daniel's promotion to chief of the wise men.

4.1 Promotion to Chief of the Wise Men

4.1.1 An Unlikely Ascent to Influence

Daniel's appointment as chief of the wise men defied conventional career trajectories, for he was a foreigner and recent exile in an elite circle dominated by long-standing Babylonian sages. His rise illustrates how competence fused with character can vault newcomers into positions of influence when established authorities fail to deliver results. Nebuchadnezzar's desperation for dream interpretation underscored the limitations of human advisors, opening a niche that Daniel filled by combining theological devotion with intellectual rigor. His medical, administrative, and linguistic training under the Chaldean curriculum provided technical credibility, yet it was his prayer-fueled insights that distinguished him in the royal eye. This unlikely ascent challenges professionals today to invest equally in skill development and spiritual formation, preparing for leadership openings when others falter. Daniel's trajectory also spotlights the role of timing: his readiness coincided with a crisis that rendered established experts helpless. Modern leaders can learn from this by maintaining continuous preparation—updating competencies and deepening devotion—so that when unexpected vacancies or emergencies arise, they stand poised to serve. Moreover, Daniel's willingness to step into an intimidating court context reveals that stepping beyond comfort zones is often necessary for exponential impact. His ascent underlines that influence in public spheres seldom results from scripted succession plans but frequently emerges when principled innovators capitalize on moments of institutional need. As we consider how Daniel stewarded his newfound authority, we turn to the practices that safeguarded integrity amid the temptations of power.

4.1.2 Stewarding Authority without Compromise

Upon receiving his royal commission, Daniel treated authority as a trust rather than a privilege, stewarding influence through policies that reflected both administrative acumen and moral conviction. He oversaw the wise men's office, likely managing budgets, setting interpretive protocols, and training subordinates in astrological methods, all while resisting any coercion to integrate pagan rites into official reports. When court ceremonies demanded invocations to Babylon's gods, Daniel upheld truth by invoking Yahweh's name or using neutral language to avoid idolatrous formulas. This careful navigation preserved his witness without fracturing professional relationships. He demonstrated that authority need not equate to coercive power; instead, it can function as a platform for ethical role modeling. Implementing transparent decision-making processes, Daniel invited colleagues to examine evidence and logic rather than accept pronouncements through intimidation. In modern terms, this looks like publishing meeting minutes, inviting stakeholder input, and setting clear accountability metrics. Daniel's refusal to exploit confidential information for personal gain further showcased how authority and integrity can coexist. He allocated promotions and honors not based on favoritism but on demonstrated merit and faithfulness, reinforcing a culture of fair opportunity. Such stewardship prevented envy and backlash by creating predictable governance norms that valued justice over expediency. When challenges arose—such as when rivals attempted to discredit him—Daniel's track record of moral consistency provided resilience, demonstrating that uncompromised authority builds institutional trust that defies circumstantial attacks. His example offers a template for leaders today to wield authority as a sacred stewardship that advances the common good without collateral spiritual compromise.

4.1.3 Navigating Pagan Workplace Ethics

Babylonian courts blended civil and religious functions, making compliance with imperial feasts, oath-sworn proclamations, and temple ceremonies unavoidable. Daniel's task was to participate in public duties—drafting decrees, advising on legal matters, and attending royal banquets—without endorsing deities that conflicted with his covenant. He navigated workplace ethics by distinguishing between civic obligations and covert liturgies of idolatry, choosing to fulfil civic duties faithfully while abstaining from overt idol worship. For instance, when decrees required invocations of Babylon's protective spirits, he likely offered silent prayers to Yahweh or used diplomatic phrasing that fulfilled legal form without theological assent. This strategy parallels modern professionals who negotiate workplace mandates—such as team-building activities or corporate messaging—that conflict with personal convictions. By seeking accommodations—like requesting alternative assignments or offering to recite shared values in more neutral terms—Daniel exemplified creative fidelity. His approach relied on respectful dialogue rather than confrontational resistance, showing that protecting conscience need not fracture workplace harmony. He also built alliances with sympathetic officials—such as Ashpenaz—who respected his skill and character, creating pockets of support that buffered him during ethical stand-offs. Daniel's navigation of pagan ethics culminated in policies that safeguarded minority practices, hinting at provisions for exiles to maintain their dietary and worship routines. These precedents laid foundations for later religious-liberty principles, demonstrating that pragmatic arrangements can uphold pluralism without betraying core convictions. His experience encourages modern believers to map institutional ethical landscapes carefully, identifying which demands are non-negotiable and where room for principled compromise exists. This nuanced navigation maintains integrity while fostering constructive collaboration in pluralistic settings.

4.1.4 Building Collaborative Teams of Integrity

Recognizing that influence multiplies through others, Daniel elevated Hananiah, Mishael, and Azariah into leadership roles, creating a collaborative team of interpreters whose shared convictions anchored collective action. By promoting colleagues who had proven fidelity in earlier trials, he underscored that trustworthiness outweighs technical prowess when shaping institutional culture. He structured workflows to ensure collective accountability, inviting team members to review each other's analyses and interpretations before presenting to the king. This peer-review model not only improved accuracy but also prevented concentration of power in a single individual—safeguarding against corruption and burnout. Daniel's team likely held regular gatherings for prayer and brainstorming, integrating communal devotion with analytical rigor. Such gatherings reinforced unity and offered mutual encouragement when facing high-stakes assignments. He invested in mentoring practices, guiding his colleagues in both Chaldean scholarship and covenantal distinctiveness, ensuring succession planning rooted in shared values. The team's collaborative ethos contrasted with Babylonian court intrigue, demonstrating that cohesive units rooted in trust outperformed fragmented rivals. Modern leaders can replicate this by forming cross-functional teams committed to ethical standards, codifying shared values in charters, and fostering environments where dissenting perspectives are welcomed. Collaborative teams of integrity become institutional guardians, capable of resisting unethical shortcuts and sustaining mission focus. Daniel's example affirms that leadership is not a solo endeavor but a communal enterprise that thrives when integrity is institutionalized through shared structures and spiritual solidarity.

4.1.5 Guarding Humility in Seasons of Honor

As Daniel accrued honors and territorial grants, he faced the perennial temptation to equate status with divine favor, risking spiritual complacency or pride. To guard humility, he sustained disciplines that kept him rooted in dependence on God—daily prayer rhythms, corporate confession sessions, and discreet acts of service to exiles in need. He publicly attributed every success to Yahweh's wisdom, ensuring that kings and officials linked breakthroughs not to human skill but to the living God. Daniel also practiced intentional anonymity in certain contexts, stepping aside to let colleagues receive credit for collaborative initiatives, thereby preventing ego-inflation. His regular reflection on past failures—such as moments of initial fear when facing royal decrees—kept him mindful of unmerited grace. He engaged in servant leadership tasks: arranging relief supplies, mediating disputes among exiles, and mentoring young officials, reminding himself that true greatness emerges through humble service (Mark 9:35). When bestowed with new responsibilities, he paused to pray before accepting, discerning whether the assignment aligned with divine calling rather than human ambition. Periodic fasts and retreats provided spiritual recalibration, preventing prestige from distorting priorities. Daniel's lifestyle demonstrated that sustained influence requires a posture of teachability, acknowledging that even seasoned advisors need correction and renewal. By modeling humble excellence, Daniel inspired both subordinates and superiors to pursue collective success over personal acclaim. His vigilance in seasons of honor preserved his witness, enabling him to serve with integrity across decades and dynastic changes. These practices illustrate how leaders today can guard humility amid accolades, ensuring that honor amplifies faithfulness rather than breeding entitlement.

4.2 Interpreting Dreams and Shaping Policy

4.2.1 The Multi-Metal Statue—Theology of Successive Kingdoms

Nebuchadnezzar's dream of a colossal statue composed of gold, silver, bronze, iron, and clay offers a compressed history of empires rising and falling under divine orchestration (Daniel 2:31–45). Daniel interpreted each element as symbolic of successive world powers—Babylon, Medo-Persia, Greece, Rome, and the fractured dominions that would follow—revealing that human glory, however lustrous, is inherently transient. This theology of kingdoms reframes geopolitical ambitions as subordinate to the Ancient of Days, whose immutable reign transcends chronologies. Daniel's exposition dismantled imperial hubris by declaring that gold heads collapse under a stone "cut not by human hands," echoing prophetic promises of a Messianic kingdom that brings justice and endures forever. This vision informed his policy recommendations, reminding rulers that long-term stability requires policies aligned with enduring moral principles rather than short-term interests. By situating economic planning within an eschatological horizon, he advocated for investments in infrastructure and social welfare that anticipated future crises rather than merely celebrating current prosperity. This theological lens also provided solace to marginalized populations, conveying that no empire, however mighty, holds ultimate authority. In modern policy contexts, a theology of successive powers encourages leaders to pursue transEpochal values—human dignity, environmental stewardship, intergenerational equity—rather than slavishly chasing GDP growth or partisan victory. Daniel's interpretation illustrates that geopolitical analysis gains depth when integrated with theological anthropology, revealing the ultimate purposes that human polities serve.

4.2.2 Translating Revelation into Public Policy

Bridging the gap between visionary insight and concrete legislation demands both translation skills and political savvy. Daniel took the abstract dream and crafted actionable counsel, advising Nebuchadnezzar—and later Darius—on how to prepare for the rise and fall of kingdoms. He likely recommended diplomatic alliances to navigate shifting power balances, economic diversification to avoid overreliance on single trade routes, and cultural programs that fostered civic identity rooted in justice. His policy briefs would have cited both historical precedents and divine warnings, blending narrative with statute to persuade skeptical advisors. He framed reforms as pragmatic necessities—encouraging rulers to heed cycles of boom and bust illustrated by the statue's metals—thus making theological convictions accessible to secular administrations. Modern policymakers can follow this model by convening interdisciplinary teams that include ethicists alongside economists and sociologists, ensuring that legislation emerges from both data and moral vision. Legislative drafts then echo theological insights: progressive taxation reflects biblical care for the poor (Leviticus 25), environmental regulations mirror stewardship mandates (Genesis 2:15), and judicial reforms embody covenantal justice (Deuteronomy 16:18–20). Daniel's example underscores that implementation plans must include stakeholder education, transparent communication, and monitoring mechanisms, transforming revelation into sustainable policy.

4.2.3 Economic Forecasting and Disaster Mitigation

Understanding the symbolic sequence of the statue's metals enabled Daniel to anticipate periods of imperial overextension and internal division. He likely advised Nebuchadnezzar to create grain reserves in years of plenty, drawing parallels to Joseph's storage strategy in Egypt (Genesis 41), thus preventing famine-induced unrest. He may have recommended infrastructure investments—canals, fortifications, and way stations—that facilitated trade and military logistics while providing employment during economic downturns. His dual insight into spiritual and material cycles offered a holistic approach to disaster mitigation, integrating prophetic warnings with pragmatic preparation. Daniel's forecasts would have included caution against speculative bubbles—paralleling the brittle clay of the statue's feet—and advocacy for diversified economies to withstand external shocks. He likely counseled on equitable taxation, balancing state revenue needs with protections for vulnerable populations. Modern analogues involve climate-resilient agriculture, strategic petroleum reserves, and financial safeguards against market crashes, all grounded in wisdom traditions that value foresight and communal responsibility. Daniel's model demonstrates that combining divine insight with empirical data produces robust contingency plans that save lives and stabilize societies.

4.2.4 Crisis Communication and Diplomatic Counsel

Delivering unwelcome news to monarchs demands rhetorical skill and relational trust. Daniel approached Nebuchadnezzar with deference, framing his interpretation as divine disclosure rather than human conjecture, thus disarming skepticism. He provided context for the dream's message, explaining the symbolic meaning before naming socioeconomic implications, thereby ensuring that rulers grasped both theological import and policy relevance. His diplomatic tone balanced candor with compassion, warning of impending judgments while offering paths to restoration through humility and justice (Daniel 4:27). In subsequent reigns, Daniel likely advised ambassadors and princes on negotiating treaties, using his understanding of imperial transitions to shape alliances that protected exiles and promoted peace. His communication style modeled the Davidic ideal of "speaking truth in love" (Ephesians 4:15), preventing panic and fostering constructive responses. Modern crisis communication teams can draw from Daniel's example by issuing clear briefings that combine transparency about risks with actionable recommendations, thus maintaining public confidence. Diplomatic counsel rooted in ethical conviction and cultural sensitivity advances negotiation outcomes, demonstrating that integrity in messaging underpins sustainable agreements.

4.2.5 Prophetic Checks on Royal Hubris

Daniel's interpretations functioned as prophetic checks, interrupting royal self-exaltation with reminders of divine oversight. When Nebuchadnezzar boasted of Babylon's everlasting grandeur, Daniel's exposition of the statue warned that pride precedes downfall (Daniel 4:28–31). He later rebuked Belshazzar's sacrilegious feast with stark declarations of impending judgment (Daniel 5), holding the king to account for his actions. These interventions exemplify prophetic courage, showing that interpreters must not shy from confronting power with inconvenient truths. Daniel balanced rebuke with hope, offering pathways for repentance that could avert or mitigate consequences. His approach maintained respect for the office while refusing to gloss over moral failings. Modern policy advisers and lobbyists can emulate this by providing honest impact assessments—highlighting ethical and long-term risks of proposed legislation regardless of political popularity. Establishing formal review panels or ethics committees, modeled after Daniel's stewardship structures, institutionalizes checks on unchecked authority. Such mechanisms prevent hubris-driven policymaking, anchoring governance in accountability to higher moral standards. Daniel's prophetic checks remind leaders that true statesmanship includes the humility to submit to transcendent norms and the courage to call peers back when they stray.

4.3 Integrity under Scrutiny—Political Jealousy and Court Intrigue

4.3.1 The Inevitable Rise of Envy

Envy often germinates in the fertile soil of comparative success, and Daniel's rapid ascent in the Babylonian court naturally provoked jealous resistance among established counselors. Those who had long enjoyed proximity to power saw their own influence wane as foreign wisdom eclipsed domestic expertise. Envy, Scripture warns, "rots the bones" (Proverbs 14:30), corroding not only relationships but also institutional trust. In Daniel's case, envy manifested in false charges and covert plotting, illustrating that high integrity can become a lightning rod for politically advantaged rivals. The jealous counselors weaponized administrative regulations—such as the decree on prayer—to engineer Daniel's downfall, showing how legalism can cloak malice in procedurals. Their envy-driven tactics echo the Pharisees' resentment of Christ's popularity (Matthew 27:18), reminding readers that religious or professional literacy does not immunize one from human sin. Envy also corrodes the envier's own soul, leaving behind bitterness that impairs judgment and sows division. To withstand this, Daniel maintained a posture of compassionate endurance, refusing to retaliate even when given the chance. He trusted that divine justice, not human schemes, would ultimately vindicate the righteous (Psalm 37:1–2). By modeling gracious restraint, he demonstrated that integrity under fire has a witness effect: some observers saw through the envy to the character beneath and were moved to confess God's greatness. Modern parallels abound: professionals whose ethical excellence threatens corrupt colleagues may face subtle ostracism, overly harsh performance reviews, or exclusion from decision-making circles. Recognizing the inevitability of envy shifts the focus from avoiding success to preparing spiritually and strategically for pushback. Daniel's response encourages contemporary leaders to cultivate inner peace through ongoing confession and prayer, preventing envy's toxic spread and sustaining institutional unity.

4.3.2 Transparency, Due Process, and Record-Keeping

When rivals deploy envy to undermine integrity, transparency serves as a powerful antidote. Daniel insisted on open procedures for dream interpretation and policy drafting, keeping meticulous records of each step—from initial consultations to final memoranda. These records functioned like modern audit trails, ensuring that decisions could be traced back to objective criteria rather than personal whim. His appeals to Darius for a public review of the prayer decree followed the biblical principle of fair hearing (Deuteronomy 25:1), demonstrating that due process preserves justice when envy-fueled accusations arise. By inviting scrutiny, Daniel turned potential ambushes into forums where truth prevailed and falsehoods were exposed. The stewardship of records also protected subordinates, as documentation showed that any collaborative work adhered to ethical standards. Contemporary public servants and corporate officers can adopt similar measures: publishing minutes, logging advisory memos, and establishing ombudsman offices to investigate complaints impartially. These practices build organizational resilience by signaling that no decision rests on secrecy and that all parties have recourse to review. Transparency need not become mere window dressing; when coupled with genuine access to information, it deters envy-driven plots by making covert manipulation more difficult. Daniel's approach underscores that integrity under scrutiny does not shrink from public exposure but leverages it to reinforce accountability and institutional credibility.

4.3.3 Ethical Whistleblowing without Weaponizing Truth

There are moments when concealment of wrongdoing is itself an injustice, and ethical whistleblowing becomes a necessary act of conscience. Daniel faced a comparable dilemma when petitioning against the prayer ban that threatened his life; his refusal to comply became a public rebuke of an unjust law. Yet he avoided the trap of weaponizing truth as a tool for power grabs, instead framing his stand as loyalty to a higher covenant. His appeals were measured, respectful of the king's office even as he refused its illegitimate demands (Daniel 6:10). This balance between candor and courtesy preserved his moral authority, preventing his act of dissent from devolving into mere personal vendetta. Modern whistleblowers can learn from this model by documenting infractions, seeking internal redress first, and framing disclosures in terms of common good rather than personal gain. Ethical whistleblowing rests on demonstrating fidelity to organizational mission—much as Daniel's protest underscored fidelity to imperial service within covenantal boundaries. When disclosures become necessary, following proper channels, providing clear evidence, and maintaining professional demeanor prevent truth-telling from becoming unethical aggression. Daniel's example shows that courageous speech born of devotion can correct institutional sin while preserving relationships and maximizing the impact of reform.

4.3.4 Compassion toward Rivals and Opponents

Even as Daniel endured schemes designed to destroy him, he maintained compassion toward his adversaries, refusing to rejoice in their failure or pray for their ruin. His intercessory prayers likely included pleas for the enlightenment of pagan counselors and the conversion of proud rulers—echoing Christ's command to love enemies (Matthew 5:44). This posture of compassion disarmed hostility over time, as some observers recognized that Daniel's motives transcended personal advantage. His capacity to pray for his accusers models the biblical mandate to "bless those who persecute you" (Romans 12:14). Compassion also preserved his own soul from bitterness, enabling him to remain effective in counsel rather than being sidetracked by revenge plots. Contemporary leaders caught in court intrigues can mirror this approach by offering mentorship or mediated dialogue to opponents, seeking common ground and shared purpose. Acts of kindness—public acknowledgment of rivals' contributions or private notes of appreciation—soften hardened hearts and build relational goodwill. Compassionate engagement, combined with unwavering commitment to truth, demonstrates that integrity need not be cold rigidity but can be warm and reconciling.

4.3.5 Resilience in Prolonged Political Storms

Enduring repeated attacks requires resilience that outlasts short-term crises. Daniel's life spanned several reigns, and he faced multiple deportations, regime changes, and renewed decrees against his practices. His sustained effectiveness emerged from rhythms of renewal—annual fasting, seasonal retreats, and communal worship with fellow exiles. These renewal practices operated like institutional sabbath cycles, preventing moral burnout and decision fatigue. He also maintained long-term vision anchored in God's unchanging promises, trusting that empires rise and fall but God's kingdom endures (Daniel 2:44). Contemporary leaders facing prolonged political storms need similar sustainability plans: mental health support, peer coaching, and periodic sabbaticals to reflect and recharge. Emotional resilience is fortified by a theology of suffering that sees hardship as refining rather than punishing (1 Peter 1:6–7). By embedding resilience practices into organizational culture—such as mandatory rest periods and peer debriefings—institutions equip leaders to withstand envy, intrigue, and shifting agendas without compromising integrity. Daniel's example offers a blueprint for sustaining mission amid tumult, demonstrating that steadfast devotion and strategic renewal combine to outlast every political tempest.

4.4 Integrating Faith and Vocation Today

4.4.1 A Theology of Work for Public Servants and Professionals

Work occupies a central place in God's creational design, as humanity was tasked to "fill the earth and subdue it" (Genesis 1:28). Daniel's tenure in Babylon illustrates that secular roles—administrators, advisors, interpreters—bear sacred significance when conducted as acts of worship. His vocational identity was not a parallel track to faith but an integrated expression of devotion, demonstrating that spreadsheets, statutes, and strategy sessions can become liturgies offered to the Creator (Colossians 3:23). Modern professionals often live compartmentalized lives, separating "spiritual" and "secular" activities, but Daniel's life affirms that every sphere falls under Christ's lordship. Theology of work encourages public servants to approach policy briefs and budget hearings with prayerful preparation, viewing each deliverable as a means to reflect God's justice and creativity. This vision combats the notion that vocation is merely a paycheck or résumé builder; instead, work is a primary context for incarnational witness, showing neighbors the dignity of labor shaped by divine design.

4.4.2 Redemptive Participation in Public Institutions

Rather than withdrawing from flawed institutions, Daniel chose redemptive engagement—working within Babylon's bureaucracy to reform practices and uphold justice. He saw public office not as a polluted pond but as a potential conduit for God's transformative purposes. His policy advising included measures that protected the vulnerable—such as guaranteeing fair treatment for exiles and promoting equitable resource distribution—reflecting prophetic mandates for social justice (Micah 6:8). Modern believers can emulate this approach by joining city councils, civil service, and nonprofit boards, bringing gospel values to budget allocations, zoning laws, and education policies. Redemptive participation recognizes that institutions carry inherited dysfunctions, yet through faithful insiders, systemic healing can begin. It requires patience, long-term commitment, and a willingness to speak truth to power—and to listen to the needs of affected communities. Daniel's cumulative impact in court demonstrates that small policy shifts, sustained over time, yield significant cultural renewal.

4.4.3 Excellence of Skill as Missional Witness

Daniel's standout proficiency in languages, mathematics, and dream interpretation served as a missional billboard, directing credit to Yahweh's wisdom rather than his own abilities. Excellence in one's craft opens doors of influence and earns social capital that can be leveraged for gospel witness. Professionals in modern contexts—engineers, doctors, educators—who pursue rigorous training and continual development reflect God's character as Creator of complexity and order. Their competence facilitates service-based witness, as colleagues trust their counsel and view their integrity as credible testimony. Excellence also counters stereotypes of faith as anti-intellectual or secondary to secular expertise. When believers demonstrate competence rooted in convictions, they invite curiosity about the Source of their strength and perseverance. Daniel's embrace of discipline and lifelong learning challenges contemporary practitioners to invest in both technical mastery and spiritual formation, ensuring that skill and character advance hand in hand.

4.4.4 Ethical Frameworks for Secular Workplaces

Secular workplaces often lack clear moral guardrails, making individual conscience the primary check against unethical behavior. Daniel implicitly employed an ethical framework guided by Torah principles—justice for the "sojourner," honesty in commerce, and protection of life. He refused bribes and insider manipulation, even when such gains might have secured personal favor. Modern employees can codify similar frameworks by developing personal codes of conduct—decision grids that reference core values and non-negotiables rooted in biblical ethics. Conscience clauses in contracts, developed in partnership with legal teams, provide formal accommodations for faith-based convictions. Workplace ethics committees, inspired by Daniel's transparent record-keeping, can serve as forums for addressing dilemmas before they escalate. Training programs that integrate case studies of Daniel's stands—his refusal of imperial food, his challenge to sacrilegious worship—equip staff to navigate ambiguous situations. Embedding ethical frameworks into performance reviews and organizational charters institutionalizes integrity, ensuring that Daniel-like convictions inform corporate culture.

4.4.5 Spiritual Disciplines Tailored for Professionals

Busy professionals require devotional practices adapted to compressed schedules and high-pressure environments. Following Daniel's example, modern practitioners might adopt "commuter prayers," using transit time for breath prayers or Scripture listening. "Meeting liturgies" infuse short pauses before discussions with a pray-for-wisdom moment, sanctifying decision-making. Quarterly "strategic retreats," even if only half-day off-site gatherings, create space for collective visioning anchored in God's promises. Regular "digital sabbaths" protect weekly rhythms of rest, ensuring that productivity does not eclipse renewal (Exodus 20:8–11). Office prayer corners—quiet nooks with devotional materials—encourage brief personal encounters with God. Lunch breaks can become "Sabbaths lite," with Scripture reading apps guiding meditative reflection. Journals kept at workstations invite spontaneous gratitude and confession, maintaining inner alignment. These tailored disciplines weave Daniel's devotional blueprint into professional contexts, fostering resilience and wisdom amid vocational demands.

4.5 Contemporary Case Studies—Modern "Daniels" in Government, Business, and NGOs

4.5.1 Anti-Corruption Prosecutors Confronting Systemic Bribery

In nations where graft undermines public trust, anti-corruption prosecutors embody Daniel's legacy by combining legal acumen with unwavering integrity. Like Daniel's refusal of illicit incentives, these lawyers pursue cases against powerful figures despite personal risk. Their work often begins with painstaking evidence-gathering—testimony, financial forensics, document audits—mirroring Daniel's meticulous record-keeping to expose clandestine schemes. Operating under threats of retaliation, they adopt spiritual disciplines—early-morning reflection, prayer circles, and written confessions—to sustain courage when facing death threats or career blacklisting. Their convictions attract support from civil-society coalitions, creating collaborative networks that reinforce each other's resolve. Convictions secured in court become lodestars of hope, demonstrating that rule of law can prevail over systemic rot. These modern "Daniels" testify that public service infused with devotion confers transformative impact, restoring faith in institutions once deemed irredeemable.

4.5.2 Data-Privacy Architects Shaping Humane Technology Policies

As algorithms increasingly govern social interaction and commerce, data-privacy architects stand at the frontlines of ethical innovation. They design and advocate for policies that protect personal dignity and guard against exploitative surveillance—issues resonant with Daniel's challenge to resist subtle forms of coercion. Their work involves interpreting complex technical "dreams" of machine learning outputs and translating them into transparent regulations that serve the public good. By convening interdisciplinary teams—programmers, legal experts, ethicists—they forge collaborative frameworks akin to Daniel's leadership of wise men teams. Spiritual disciplines—digital sabbaths, corporate prayer huddles, and sabbatical residencies—equip these professionals to discern ethical boundaries when tempted by proprietary data gains. Their policies, once implemented, safeguard vulnerable populations and promote equitable access to digital services. In doing so, they fulfill a modern iteration of Daniel's mission: steering powerful systems in alignment with transcendent moral imperatives.

4.5.3 Healthcare Executives Advocating for Underserved Populations

Healthcare systems worldwide grapple with disparities in access and quality of care. Executives who champion equity initiatives echo Daniel's stand for minority rights in exile. They leverage administrative influence to allocate resources for rural clinics, mobile health units, and telemedicine programs, ensuring that underserved communities receive life-saving treatments. Their leadership teams adopt corporate liturgies—regular prayer breakfasts, ethics rounds, and reflective quality-improvement sessions—that integrate spiritual convictions with operational planning. They resist cost-cutting measures that compromise patient dignity, drawing on a theology of compassion rooted in Jeremiah's call to "seek the welfare" of foreign lands (Jeremiah 29:7). Through transparent policies and community partnerships, they build trust among populations historically marginalized by medical institutions. These modern "Daniels" demonstrate that vocational excellence, when coupled with devout compassion, yields systemic transformation in public health outcomes.

4.5.4 Diplomatic Envoys Mediating Peace with Faith-Rooted Empathy

Diplomats tasked with brokering peace in conflict zones often operate under immense pressure, similar to Daniel's role mediating between warring kingdoms. Envoys who ground their approach in prayerful preparation and covenantal empathy create space for genuine dialogue. They listen attentively to divergent narratives, offering nonviolent proposals that respect each party's dignity. Their mediation teams include chaplains and spiritual advisors, integrating contemplative pauses into negotiation schedules to prevent reactive rhetoric. By modeling foot-washing humility—serving all sides with impartial compassion—they build relational trust reminiscent of Daniel's gracious service to successive monarchs. Their peace accords, when codeveloped with local faith communities, achieve greater durability, reflecting the synergy of political savvy and spiritual wisdom. These diplomatic "Daniels" reveal that devotion-informed service can reconcile ancient enmities and usher in fragile yet hopeful eras of stability.

4.6 The Liturgy of Leadership—Practices that Sustain Integrity

4.6.1 Weekly Examen for Decision-Makers

Leaders who navigate complex responsibilities benefit from a structured practice of reflection known as the Examen, adapted from Ignatian spirituality, which invites them to review the week's decisions through four movements: gratitude, petition, review, and hope. Starting with gratitude, leaders recall specific moments of blessing—successful collaborations, moments of clarity, or simple encouragement from colleagues—to cultivate a posture of thankfulness that counters entitlement. In the petition phase, they ask for deeper insight into unresolved dilemmas and for God's continued guidance, acknowledging their dependence rather than treating wisdom as a self-generated commodity (James 1:5). The review movement examines the week's choices—policies enacted, emails sent, meetings chaired—asking whether each aligned with justice, mercy, and humility (Micah 6:8). Leaders note successes and missteps alike, discerning patterns of overreaction to pressure or negligence of empathy. This review surfaces hidden idols—status, efficiency, approval—that subtly shaped decisions, paving the way for confession and repentance. Finally, in the hope movement, leaders look forward, interceding for upcoming negotiations and trusting that God can transform past mistakes into future growth (Romans 8:28). Conducted in solitude or with a trusted mentor, the weekly Examen institutionalizes reflection, preventing the moral drift that accompanies nonstop action. It transforms time into a sacred space where leaders offer their victories and failures back to the One who ordains seasons. Over time, this ritual fosters resilient self-awareness, sharpening the moral imagination needed for high-stakes governance. The Examen also models teachable leadership: by admitting blind spots, leaders invite collective accountability and inspire teams to pursue shared integrity.

4.6.2 Public Confession of Conflicts of Interest

Transparency in leadership requires more than private integrity; it demands proactive disclosure of factors that might compromise objectivity. Public confession of potential conflicts of interest—financial investments, familial affiliations, or external alliances—preempts suspicion and builds trust. In Daniel's context, he might have disclosed ties to fellow exiles or shared familial bonds, ensuring that his counsel to kings was never misconstrued as self-serving. Modern leaders can adopt similar practices by publishing conflict matrices alongside policy briefings, highlighting any personal stakes that warrant recusal or mitigation. This openness invites public scrutiny and reduces the influence of hidden pressures that can derail decisions. Confession also models vulnerability, encouraging team members to disclose their own potential conflicts without fear of shame. By normalizing these disclosures in staff meetings, boards, and public addresses, organizations signal that ethical lapses, rather than the confession of conflicts, pose the greater risk. Regular updates to conflict registries—quarterly or annually—ensure that new relationships or investments are promptly addressed. Public confession extends beyond proscribed categories, encompassing biases and preferences that might color judgment. Leaders can facilitate workshops on unconscious bias, creating forums where colleagues collaboratively explore and confess hidden influences. Such practices transform confession from an admission of guilt into a communal commitment to integrity, aligning institutional culture with covenantal accountability.

4.6.3 Rhythms of Retreat, Mentorship, and Intercessory Teams

Sustained integrity requires cycles of withdrawal, guidance, and collective prayer that replenish spiritual and emotional resources. Retreats—whether overnight or weeklong—create intentional distance from daily demands, allowing leaders to recalibrate vision, refresh devotion, and receive pastoral care. Retreat settings might include silent reflection, guided Scripture meditations, and communal worship, mirroring Daniel's withdrawals for intercession before critical court encounters. Mentorship relationships supplement retreats by providing ongoing feedback, wisdom, and encouragement; mentors, ideally more seasoned, help protégés apply devotional insights to complex challenges. These dyadic bonds foster growth through mutual accountability, as mentors both challenge ambition and affirm vocational calling. Intercessory teams—small groups of prayer partners—surround leaders with spiritual support, covering them in regular petitions for wisdom, courage, and protection. These teams meet weekly, share confidential updates on looming decisions, and intercede both privately and corporately, embodying the mutual solidarity Daniel found with his friends (Daniel 2:16–18). The interplay of solitude, mentorship, and intercession prevents isolation, sustains emotional equilibrium, and buffers leaders against the corrosive effects of power. Institutions can formalize these rhythms by allotting dedicated retreat times in annual calendars, pairing emerging leaders with trained mentors, and establishing prayer cohorts with rotating membership. By embedding these practices into governance structures, organizations honor the truth that public service flourishes only when rooted in communal care and consistent renewal.

4.6.4 Financial Transparency and Simplicity as Safeguards against Greed

Accumulative wealth can erode integrity and precipitate conflicts of interest, yet leaders often rationalize personal enrichment as a just reward for service. Daniel, by contrast, accepted material rewards—high office and land—while avoiding ostentatious displays or personal gain at others' expense. He remained keenly aware of the biblical warnings against the love of money, which "is a root of all kinds of evil" (1 Timothy 6:10). Modern leaders protect against greed through financial transparency: publishing compensation packages, expense reports, and organizational budgets for stakeholder review. Simplicity—adopting modest lifestyles rather than lavish perks—models restraint and solidarity with those served. Policies such as capped benefits, standardized travel protocols, and ethically vetted vendors prevent the slide into indulgence. Regular audits by independent bodies ensure compliance and deter misuse of resources. Transparency coupled with simplicity signals that organizational resources exist to advance mission rather than personal enrichment. Scriptures like Acts 4:32–35, which describe early believers sharing possessions, inspire communal generosity models where surpluses support social programs and mission initiatives. Leaders who commit to donate a portion of their income to charitable causes demonstrate personal alignment with institutional values. These financial practices function as liturgical acts: offerings of tangible assets that sanctify material resources under divine sponsorship. By weaving financial transparency and simplicity into organizational norms, institutions create robust safeguards against the corrosive temptations of wealth and power.

4.7 Fiery Faith in the Furnace of Public Opinion

4.7.1 How Sustained Integrity Invites Both Divine Favor and Cultural Backlash

The consistent exercise of integrity, modeled by Daniel across successive regimes, naturally drew divine favor as evidenced by miraculous deliverances and royal commendations (Daniel 6:22–23). His unwavering faithfulness prompted edicts that honored Yahweh and protected exiles, illustrating that God cares for those who honor Him amid hostile environments. Yet the same integrity that elicited heavenly rescue also incited jealousy and lethal decrees, as when rivals manipulated Darius into banning Daniel's prayer (Daniel 6:7). This dual effect—divine vindication coupled with intensified opposition—highlights that steadfast devotion rarely renders a smooth path. Instead, it catalyzes both blessing and backlash, exposing countercultural convictions to the heat of public scrutiny. Cultural backlash emerges when societal norms collide with uncompromising ethics, manifesting as social ostracism, legislative penalties, or smear campaigns. Leaders who practice sustained integrity should anticipate such reprisals, viewing them not as failures but as markers of faithful witness (Matthew 5:10–12). Historical examples include civil-rights activists lauded by some and vilified by others, or whistleblowers commended for courage yet sanctioned by institutions. Recognizing that divine favor and cultural backlash often go hand in hand prepares leaders to endure public opinion's furnace with resilience. It also underscores the importance of the spiritual rhythms—prayer, retreat, confession—outlined in this chapter, which sustain conviction when external pressures mount. As we transition to the next chapter, we will see how Hananiah, Mishael, and Azariah embodied this fiery faith by facing literal flames rather than compromising worship.

4.7.2 Previewing Hananiah, Mishael, and Azariah's Confrontation with Totalitarian Idolatry

Following Daniel's example in the lion's den, his three friends set a precedent for collective fidelity when faced with a command to worship an imperial image or perish in a blazing furnace (Daniel 3:1–6). Their story illustrates how corporate solidarity amplifies individual courage, as they refused to bow even when threatened with immediate execution. The narrative spotlights their strategic nonviolent resistance, their surrender of personal safety for covenant loyalty, and the miraculous intercession of the "fourth man" in the fire. Their ordeal demonstrates that some forms of idolatry—state-mandated worship, conflation of national identity with religious practice—demand unwavering refusal, even at the cost of life. Their deliverance, culminating in senior leadership's public declaration praising the "God who saves," exemplifies the fusion of private conviction and public vindication. As readers embark on Chapter 5, they will witness how the convictions nurtured in Chapters 1–4 prepare believers for ultimate tests of loyalty that transcend personal comfort and professional security.

4.7.3 Invitation to Readers to Audit Their Own Spheres of Influence

Before confronting literal furnaces or modern equivalents—such as hostile legislation, hostile media, or workplace mandates that conflict with conscience—readers are encouraged to conduct an integrity audit of their own environments. This audit involves identifying areas where concessions have been made for convenience, labeling potential modern "golden images" that compete for primary allegiance, and charting risks associated with uncompromised loyalty. Drawing on the spiritual disciplines and leadership liturgies described in this chapter, individuals and teams can develop contingency plans for standing firm—engaging mentors, forming intercessory allies, and preparing principled requests for accommodations. By proactively aligning devotion, vocation, and institutional engagement, readers can move into future trials not as unprepared spectators but as seasoned participants. This preparatory step ensures that when demands for compromise arise, believers will navigate them with the same wisdom, courage, and prayerful dependence that characterized Daniel and his friends, ready to testify that worship of the One True God is worth every cost.

Conclusion

Daniel's tenure in the royal courts stands as a timeless example of how devotion transforms leadership. The same disciplines that sustained him in exile—prayerful dependence, communal accountability, and ethical clarity—underwrote every moment of public responsibility, from interpreting geopolitical visions to crafting fair policies. His life reminds us that true influence arises not from maneuvering alone but from character forged before God. When envy flares and corruption beckons, the habits of humility and transparency described in this chapter become essential safeguards. As modern believers engage governing institutions, they can draw on Daniel's legacy: pursuing excellence, resisting compromise, and leveraging positions of authority to embody the justice and mercy of God's kingdom. In doing so, they discover that serving with integrity does more than preserve individual souls—it reshapes societies and points nations back to the One who reigns forever.

Chapter 5 – Fiery Faith: Hananiah, Mishael, and Azariah in the Furnace

When power demands absolute allegiance, faith faces its severest test. The furnace episode in Daniel 3 stands as a defining moment where three young exiles chose death over compromise, refusing to bow before a colossal golden idol. Their story reframes suffering not as a sign of divine absence but as the crucible in which true allegiance is revealed. In an environment engineered to crush dissent—where music, spectacle, and law fused into a potent apparatus of control—Hananiah, Mishael, and Azariah demonstrated that worship of the One True God transcends any earthly mandate. This chapter explores how their collective resistance, rooted in covenant identity and bolstered by mutual solidarity, transforms coercion into a stage for miraculous deliverance. Their example challenges every generation to discern and defy modern idols, to forge bonds of courageous community, and to embrace the hope that even the fiercest flames cannot consume hearts anchored in divine fidelity.

5.0 Crucible of Conscience—Setting the Stage for Defiant Worship

5.0.1 Neo-Babylonian Politics behind the Ninety-Foot Statue

The statue erected by Nebuchadnezzar represented more than a city's engineering prowess; it embodied the state's claim to ultimate authority over its subjects. The gold head signified the king's divine status in Babylonian theology, positioning him as the incarnation of Marduk's will on earth. Invoking such imagery before the assembled governors created a political theater in which civic allegiance morphed seamlessly into spiritual worship. Provincial leaders, satraps, and foreign nobles were compelled to internalize the message that rejecting the statue equated to rejecting the empire itself. This conflation of political loyalty and religious devotion underpinned Babylon's totalitarian governance, ensuring that dissent could be framed as sedition rather than conscience. The king's decree mandated that when the musical instruments sounded, every person—regardless of ethnicity or prior faith—must bow, illustrating how law was weaponized to enforce uniform ideology. Failure to comply invited immediate execution, a deterrent designed to suppress isolated resistance before it could coalesce. Such political dramas reinforced the notion that empire and cult were inseparable, making worship a compulsory affirmation of state power. For Hananiah, Mishael, and Azariah, the statue's presence on the Dura plain symbolized a crucible of conscience where vocational duty, civic responsibility, and covenant loyalty collided. Their decision to refuse the decree therefore carried profound political risk, challenging not only religious mandates but also the foundational structures of imperial authority. This backdrop of coercive politics sets the stage for understanding the intensity of the confrontation that follows.

5.0.2 Collective Psychology of Coerced Devotion on the Dura Plain

Mass ceremonies on the Dura plain functioned as psychological operations designed to produce what modern social scientists call "groupthink." As thousands gathered beneath the statue's gaze, peer pressure and fear of ostracism pressed the crowd toward unanimous compliance. Musicians, heralds, and courtiers amplified the spectacle, creating sensory overload that drowned out private convictions. Those who hesitated were subject to public shame, becoming cautionary examples whose plight reinforced the majority's conformity. The ritual design leveraged identity psychology: participants were made to feel that bowing expressed their inclusion in Babylon's grand narrative. Officials circulated identity tokens—medals, robes, or proclamations—that rewarded the compliant, while labeling dissenters as "other" and dehumanizing them. Such dynamics illustrate how even well-intentioned individuals can capitulate when communal rituals override personal ethics. Hananiah, Mishael, and Azariah confronted not only the king's edict but also the invisible currents of mass psychology that distort moral judgment. Their resistance broke the spell of collective conformity, demonstrating that individual agency can pierce the veil of group coercion. Observers who witnessed their stand were forced to reckon with conscience, as the trio's calm refusal exposed the hollow promises of forced unity. This collective psychology underscores the remarkable courage required to dissent publicly, highlighting the furnace as both a physical and psychological trial.

5.0.3 Linking Daniel's Courtroom Integrity to His Friends' Public Stand

Daniel's earlier acts of conscience—refusing royal delicacies and interpreting dreams with honesty—provided a foundation for his friends' later resistance. His silent witness in high office lent credibility to Hananiah, Mishael, and Azariah when they faced imperial demands, showing that covenant faithfulness could coexist with public service. Through whispered counsel and shared prayer, Daniel likely encouraged their conviction, modeling how private integrity in elite spheres translates into communal solidarity under duress. His refined reputation among officials meant that their stand, though legally indefensible, carried the weight of a broader narrative of divine fidelity. The link between Daniel's courtroom defiance and their furnace testimony illustrates how individual integrity can ripple outward, empowering others to risk everything for obedience. This dynamic also underscores the relational dimension of faith: convictions do not arise in isolation but in networks of trust and mentorship. The friends' solidarity in the face of the furnace echoes Daniel's prior refusal to bow to pragmatic compromise, demonstrating the continuity of covenant identity across different forms of crisis.

5.0.4 Eschatological Echo—Empire's Demand for Total Allegiance across the Ages

The furnace episode resonates with later biblical warnings about enforced worship in apocalyptic visions. John's Revelation portrays a time when humanity will be compelled to worship the beast's image under pains of death (Revelation 13:15), mirroring the furnace decree. This eschatological echo frames Hananiah, Mishael, and Azariah as prophetic prototypes, teaching future generations that absolute loyalty to God must supersede any human mandate. Their story anticipates a final conflict between divine sovereignty and totalitarian coercion, positioning faithful defiance as the definitive mark of discipleship. By examining their ordeal, readers glimpse the ongoing struggle against empires—ancient and modern—that demand ultimate allegiance. Their example thus extends beyond historical context, speaking to every era's "golden image" whether political ideology, mass media, or technological panopticons. Understanding this eschatological dimension prepares believers to recognize and resist present-day analogues of empire's demands, equipping them for faithful witness in the face of coercive conformity.

5.1 The Image of Gold and Imperial Idolatry

5.1.1 Anatomy of Totalitarian Worship

Imperial cults in the ancient Near East fused political and religious authority, presenting rulers as divine or semi-divine figures whose images commanded worship. Babylonian inscriptions and archaeological finds confirm that statues served as focal points for civic religion, with priests mediating between citizens and the king's deified persona. Rituals included processions, sacrificial offerings, and recitations of royal epithets equating the monarch with major deities. These liturgies reinforced the social hierarchy by framing the crowned head as the source of prosperity and security. Attendance at ceremonies was often mandatory, enforced by local governors who commanded loyalty through a combination of privilege and threat. Music, chants, and ritual gestures coalesced into a sensory experience aimed at overwhelming individual thought, producing a trance-like conformity that quelled dissent. Refusal to participate branded individuals as traitors, subjecting them to fines, exile, or execution. By controlling the narrative of divine favor, the state maintained social order and legitimized its expansionist ambitions. This architecture of worship reveals the stakes of Hananiah, Mishael, and Azariah's refusal: they contested not a mere symbol but the fusion of political power with theological claims, exposing the idolatry at the heart of the empire. Their defiance illuminated the falsity of totalitarian worship by demonstrating that a living God surpasses any human image.

5.1.2 Liturgies of Empire vs Liturgies of Yahweh

Babylonian liturgies required acts of ritual submission—bowing, incense offerings, recitations—directed toward images representing imperial deities and the king himself. These repeated enactments functioned as daily catechisms, reprogramming hearts to find ultimate meaning in civic identity. By contrast, Israelite worship centered on Yahweh's unique claims: exclusive devotion to the one true God, expressed through festivals (Passover, Pentecost), sacrificial systems, and the Shema's daily recitation (Deuteronomy 6:4–5). The posture of standing in prayer before the Lord contrasted with prostration before idols, signaling an unshakable commitment to covenant fidelity. Liturgies to Yahweh emphasized communal restoration, justice for the poor, and ethical holiness, whereas imperial rituals prioritized order, obedience, and glorification of state. The spiritual rhythms of tableside Torah readings and temple sacrifices nurtured a distinct collective identity that transcended national allegiances. When the furnace decree mandated the liturgy of empire, Hananiah, Mishael, and Azariah recognized that participating would violate the covenant's core: "You shall have no other gods before me" (Exodus 20:3). Their refusal returned worship to its covenantal center, reclaiming the liturgy as an act of allegiance to Yahweh alone. Contemporary analogues—national pledges, corporate oaths, online identity rituals—demand similar discernment, urging believers to test which liturgies shape their ultimate devotion.

5.1.3 Psychological Warfare and Minority Marginalization

Imperial rituals exploited psychological tactics to marginalize dissenters and reinforce group cohesion. Public ceremonies conveyed the message that belonging hinged on conformity; officials used rewards—honors, promotions, public accolades—to incentivize participation. Fear tactics, such as parading would-be dissidents before crowds or public executions at the statue's base, underscored that resistance carried mortal risk. Minority groups, including Jewish exiles, felt the pinch especially keenly as they had to negotiate between preserving their identity and avoiding persecution. Propaganda campaigns portrayed refusal to worship as irrational stubbornness, stigmatizing dissenters as contemptuous of communal harmony. In this context, Hananiah, Mishael, and Azariah's stance eliminated any middle ground, making them emblematic outcasts. Yet their solidarity and courage disrupted the psychological calculus: by standing together, they weakened the state's ability to isolate individuals. Their example demonstrates that communal support can blunt psychological warfare, offering a counter-narrative to state propaganda. Modern minorities facing coercive ideologies—religious, political, or corporate—encounter similar marginalization tactics, from social media cancelation to institutional blacklisting. Recognizing these psychological ploys enables faithful communities to develop resilience strategies, ensuring that dissent need not become a lonely, suicidal choice but can inspire collective defiance grounded in mutual care.

5.2 Civil Disobedience and Non-violent Resistance

5.2.1 The Decision to Remain Upright

Faced with an ultimatum to bow or die, Hananiah, Mishael, and Azariah engaged in a deliberate discernment process rooted in covenant loyalty. Their earlier experiences—refusing royal food, preserving prayer rhythms—had already taught them to weigh temporal consequences against eternal obedience. Before the decree, they likely consulted one another, recalling Jeremiah's counsel to seek Babylon's welfare while refusing its idols (Jeremiah 29:7). This collective deliberation, combined with solitary prayer, crystallized their commitment to stand upright rather than bow. Their decision entailed full awareness of potential outcomes and an embrace of risk as a testament to Yahweh's sovereignty. They modeled Jesus' teaching on civil disobedience: to obey God rather than men when institutions overstep divine mandates (Acts 5:29). Their upright stance communicated that physical postures reflect deeper spiritual realities, making the body itself an instrument of testimony. Even as the furnace's flames licked the air, their resolve remained unbent, illustrating that moral inner girding precedes external action. This decision, anchored in disciplined devotion, transformed imminent martyrdom into an act of prophetic witness whose flame outshone the literal fire.

5.2.2 Legal Fallout and Show-Trial Dynamics

The plotting counselors leveraged the new decree as a legal snare, ensnaring Daniel's friends through show-trial tactics. They appealed to Darius's esteem for Daniel by pointing out the proximity of Daniel's allies, manufacturing evidence that any compliance or non-compliance would violate the letter of the law. They exploited procedural loopholes—such as the irrevocable nature of the royal edict—to ensure that the king's hands were effectively tied once he had signed. The ensuing trial was less an inquiry than a spectacle, designed to intimidate other dissenters and affirm the state's omnipotence. The trio's defense rested not on legal technicalities but on the higher-law argument that God's commands supersede human statutes. Their refusal to engage in standard courtroom tactics—discounting bribes, bypassing appeals—exposed the hollowness of the imperial legal system. This contrast highlighted the difference between human justice, vulnerable to manipulation, and divine justice, rooted in unchanging righteousness. The episode foreshadows later Christian martyrs who faced show trials under Roman imperial law, affirming that faithfulness often appears irrational to power structures fixated on order at any cost.

5.2.3 Presence of the "Fourth Man" in Suffering

Amid the furnace's blaze, the three witnesses detected a fourth figure, described as like "a son of the gods," who accompanied them unscathed. This otherworldly presence symbolized God's intimate solidarity with the faithful in their most harrowing trials. Jewish interpreters saw echoes of Shekhinah glory, while Christian readings identified the figure prefiguratively as the preincarnate Christ (Matthew 28:2–3). The fourth man's appearance transformed the furnace from a site of destruction into a sanctuary of divine companionship, underscoring that suffering need not be solitary. His presence reassured the trio that ultimate loyalty to Yahweh does not result in abandonment but in closer communion. For modern readers, this image equips believers to perceive God's nearness in persecution and marginalization, offering assurance that no trial severs the covenant bond. The "Fourth Man" also reframes suffering: fire becomes the medium through which faith is purified and fellowship deepened. Recognizing this companionship emboldens communities to face their own "furnaces" together, confident that they are never alone.

5.3 Solidarity in Suffering—Strength in Shared Conviction

5.3.1 Communal Courage Over Individual Heroics

When Hananiah, Mishael, and Azariah faced the furnace decree together, their combined witness demonstrated that solidarity magnifies courage far beyond what a lone individual can muster. Their mutual vow to stand fast, rooted in shared prayer and covenantal memory, created an inner fortress of resolve that insulated each one from crumbling under isolation. By choosing to act as a unit, they disrupted the regime's strategy of targeting isolated resisters; their unity made it more difficult for the state to erase dissent without creating a larger scandal. Sociological studies confirm that group cohesion under risk conditions dramatically increases the likelihood of sustained non-violent resistance, as members draw strength from observing one another's steadfastness and verbal affirmations of mutual loyalty. In revisiting earlier chapters, we noted how Daniel's intercession with friends set a precedent for this solidarity, showing that spiritual alliances precede political stands. The triad's collective courage also served as a prophetic indictment of imperial ideology: by refusing to bow en masse, they proclaimed that allegiance to Yahweh transcended ethnic and national boundaries. Their solidarity resonated beyond the furnace, inspiring other exiles to seek communal support in upholding Torah ethics under foreign rule. Early church martyrdom accounts reflect a similar dynamic, where groups of believers would gather to pray before entering arenas, reinforcing one another's faith. In modern dissent movements, clandestine networks and cell structures echo this pattern, enabling participants to resist authoritarian demands through interdependent trust rather than lone-wolf action. Communal courage transforms what seems like suicidal individualism into a powerful communal witness that shakes the moral foundations of oppressive systems. The three Hebrews thus modeled how friendship rooted in spiritual conviction becomes a repository of resilience that neither state violence nor social pressure can easily breach.

5.3.2 Worship Inside the Furnace

Ancient commentators and modern scholars alike marvel at the possibility that Hananiah, Mishael, and Azariah did not merely survive the furnace but continued to worship within it. The text's lack of detail about their words or songs invites imaginative reconstruction: perhaps they recited Psalms of trust—Psalm 23's "Even though I walk through the valley of the shadow of death" or Psalm 121's "My help comes from the Lord"—embedding their fiery ordeal in covenant language. This internal act of worship transformed the furnace from a site of execution into a sanctuary, for worship consecrates space wherever God's people proclaim His name (Matthew 18:20). The presence of the "fourth man" provided divine accompaniment, but the worship itself demonstrated that liturgy can transcend physical constraints, as Stephen's vision of glory preceded his martyrdom (Acts 7:55–56). Singing or praying in flames defies natural expectations and reaffirms the conviction that spiritual realities trump physical danger. The act of worship in extremity also anticipated the early church's persecution-era hymns, such as those included in second-century apocryphal writings where believers sang psalms en route to execution. Liturgical creativity in crisis fosters solidarity, as group singing unifies hearts and wards off panic. Moreover, worship inside the furnace served as non-violent resistance to state ideologies: while the empire demanded bodily submission, song affirmed the Hebrews' inner allegiance to Yahweh alone. Contemporary believers facing digital "furnaces"—online cancelation or institutional exile—can invoke this model by using virtual liturgies and communal prayers to counteract demeaning narratives. Worship thus becomes a weapon of spiritual warfare, shifting focus from oppressive circumstances to the eternal throne. By embedding their suffering within a framework of praise, the three friends modeled faith that sees every trial as an opportunity for doxology.

5.3.3 Public Vindication and Policy Reversal

The aftermath of the furnace trial culminated in an imperial decree that praised the God of Israel and guaranteed protection for His worshipers, illustrating how faithful witness can catalyze systemic change. When Darius beheld the three figures unharmed, he issued a proclamation requiring all subjects to fear "the God of Shadrach, Meshach, and Abednego" (Daniel 3:29), effectively extending conscience protections across the empire. This policy reversal echoing earlier decrees in Daniel's career demonstrates that acts of defiant worship can reorient state religion rather than merely preserve private belief. Historians note that these decrees would have been inscribed on clay tablets and posted in public spaces, ensuring legal force and widespread awareness. Such vindications tend to follow pivotal crises; the Book of Esther similarly chronicles how a threatened people became the beneficiaries of royal edicts protecting their lives (Esther 8). Public vindication not only saved the three from execution but also opened legal space for other minorities to practice their faiths. The sequence underscores a principle: when conscience-driven defiance forces rulers to choose between coercion and credibility, states often opt for pragmatic inclusion to preserve social stability. Daniel's interpretive role likely contributed to this shift, as earlier dream interpretations had already inculcated reverence for Yahweh among Babylon's elite. Modern advocates for religious liberty draw on these precedents when lobbying for conscience clauses in legislation and constitutional protections. Legal scholars reference the furnace decree as a proto-constitutional acknowledgment of conscience rights, demonstrating that divine vindication can translate into enduring policy frameworks. Public vindication thus serves as both reward for faithfulness and a catalyst for reform, reminding believers that God's purposes extend beyond personal deliverance to societal transformation.

5.4 Modern Idols and the Cost of Loyalty

5.4.1 Nationalism Rebranded as Divine Mandate

In many societies, the flag and national anthem function as secular sacraments, demanding quasi-religious devotion that can eclipse commitments to higher moral law. Nationalism often repackages loyalty to country as a divine mandate, invoking slogans like "God and Country" to blur boundaries between civic pride and theological fidelity. These ideologies transform citizens into subjects of a civil religion, prescribing rituals—pledges, parades, mandatory oaths—that mirror the furnace liturgies of Babylon. Dissenters who refuse to stand for national anthems or recite pledges risk social sanction, job loss, or legal penalties, reflecting patterns akin to the furnace decree. Scripture offers a corrective vision, affirming that God alone is Lord of nations (Psalm 22:28) and that earthly citizenship remains subordinate to heavenly citizenship (Philippians 3:20). Prophets like Jeremiah emphasized seeking the welfare of one's city while refusing idolatrous concessions, suggesting that faithful national engagement requires both participation and prophetic critique (Jeremiah 29:7). In contexts where nationalism becomes an idol, believers must discern whether acts of civic devotion honor God or perpetuate idolatry. Solidarity with the oppressed and calls for justice can serve as acts of "fiery faith," challenging national mythologies that demand uncritical allegiance. Historical figures such as Dietrich Bonhoeffer and Martin Luther King Jr. embodied this tension, refusing to conflate patriotism with faithfulness when the nation's policies contradicted gospel imperatives. Modern disciples can follow their example by engaging in civil disobedience against laws that privilege one group over another, demonstrating that ultimate loyalty rests with God's kingdom rather than any flag. Realigning nationalism under divine Lordship protects against the furnace of forced devotion, ensuring that civic participation remains accountable to transcendent truth.

5.4.2 Consumerism's Invisible Furnace

In affluent societies, consumer culture operates as a pervasive, invisible furnace, demanding constant worship of material abundance. Advertising campaigns function like imperial decrees, commanding attention through sensory bombardment of images and slogans that equate consumption with identity, belonging, and ultimate satisfaction. Businesses deploy data-driven algorithms to predict and manipulate desires, reinforcing patterns of compulsive shopping that become daily rituals of submission to market gods. Credit systems and installment plans serve as chains that bind individuals to cyclical debt, much as the furnace's flames represent bondage to idols. Sabbath observance, once a covenant marker, dwindles under the lure of perpetual commerce and entertainment, further enslaving hearts to consumer-driven fulfillment. Biblical counsel calls for simplicity and thanksgiving (1 Timothy 6:6–10), modeling fasting from unnecessary purchases as counter-liturgies to economic idolatry. Community practices—such as clothing swaps, tool libraries, and generosity networks—reveal alternative economies that honor stewardship and mutual care. Faith-based organizations have pioneered "furnace-fast" events, where participants refrain from nonessential spending for a month, redirecting saved funds to relief efforts. Such disciplines break the cycle of craving and help communities discern genuine needs from manufactured desires. By treating consumerism as a furnace that tests loyalty, believers recover the freedom to worship God alone. These practices also cultivate gratitude and creativity, loosening the grip of acquisitive anxiety and opening space for communal solidarity.

5.4.3 Identity Politics and the Golden Self

Contemporary identity politics often elevates personal narratives and group affiliations into near-absolute categories, pressuring individuals to define themselves primarily by race, gender, or ideology. Social media platforms amplify these pressures through algorithms that curate content in echo chambers, rewarding conformity to prevailing group norms and punishing deviants with public shaming. Like the furnace decree, identity-affirming rituals—viral hashtags, solidarity marches, online pledges—become tests of loyalty, where refusal to participate brands one as an outsider. While the Bible acknowledges the value of personal stories and communal belonging, it insists that ultimate identity rests in being "new creations" in Christ (2 Corinthians 5:17). Gospel identity transcends and subsumes secondary markers, calling believers to unity as citizens of a diverse yet reconciled body (Galatians 3:28). Resisting the furnace of self-idolatry involves practices such as mutual confession of distinctive idols, cross-cultural dialogues that prioritize listening over asserting positions, and communal acts of service that cut across identity lines. Churches can host "anonymous service" events where participants serve without revealing personal demographics, underscoring that love and mercy, not identity labels, drive communal bonds. Such disciplines reveal that true dignity emerges from gospel transformation rather than from enforced groupings. As believers reclaim their foundational identity in Christ, they become witnesses to a community that celebrates diversity without mandating uniform thought or forced allegiance.

5.4.4 Counting the Cost: Vocational, Relational, Legal

Loyalty to God in facing modern idols often incurs tangible costs across multiple dimensions of life. Vocationally, professionals may lose promotions, be excluded from lucrative contracts, or even face termination for upholding covenant ethics—such as refusing to participate in discriminatory policies or manipulative marketing campaigns. Relationally, family members and peers who embrace cultural norms may distance themselves, leaving resisters to navigate social isolation. Legal ramifications can emerge when laws protect majority preferences over minority consciences, leading to fines, lawsuits, or criminal charges—paralleling the threat of the burning furnace. Historically, conscientious objectors and civil-rights activists have experienced these costs, yet their perseverance catalyzed broader legal reforms, such as protections for religious freedom and civil liberties. Believers can prepare by establishing supportive community networks—legal defense funds, mutual aid societies, and fellowship groups—that share risks and resources. Vocational planning includes crafting exit strategies and alternative income models to sustain ministries and ethical enterprises. Relationships can be fortified through intentional hospitality and dialogue, reducing alienation by building bridges of understanding even amid disagreement. Legal cost calculation involves awareness of rights, strategic use of faith-based exemptions, and alliances with civil-rights organizations. By counting these costs in advance, resisters prevent panic when trials arrive and maintain clarity about the stakes involved. Their calculated risks echo the Hebrews' walk into the furnace: a deliberate step of faith that anticipates both suffering and vindication.

5.5 Practising Fiery Faith Today—Disciplines of Defiant Worship

5.5.1 Memory Work: Rehearsing Martyr Stories and Biblical Deliverances

Cultivating readiness for defiant worship begins with memory work—deliberately recalling the testimonies of martyrs and deliverance narratives that anchor hope in God's faithfulness. Regularly reading about early church martyrs, the Reformers who faced persecution, and modern believers who endured imprisonment for conscience nurtures a sense of solidarity across centuries. This practice parallels Daniel's reflection on the exodus from Egypt and the prophets' deliverances, which fueled his courage in court. Congregational calendar events—such as "Heroes of Faith" Sundays—highlight these stories through sermons, liturgical readings, and displays in communal spaces. Personal devotion can include journaling connections between historical accounts and present trials, noting patterns of divine intervention. Quiet retreats that center on heritage meditation—listening to recorded testimonies, reading primary-source letters—create immersive experiences where memory becomes motivator. Churches might curate "remembrance walls" where believers post names and stories of those who stood for conscience. Digital platforms can host year-round "memory campaigns," sending weekly biographies and discussion prompts to subscribers. This ongoing rehearsal embeds the furnace story within believers' imaginations, priming hearts for courageous acts when idols demand worship.

5.5.2 Embodied Liturgies: Standing Prayers, Fasting from Curated Applause

Embodied liturgies translate internal convictions into visible acts that publicly align worship with God rather than cultural approval. Standing prayers—taking physical stands in public spaces or workplaces during moments that demand allegiance—mirror Hananiah, Mishael, and Azariah's upright posture. These might occur during political ceremonies, corporate rituals, or social-media campaigns that urge conformity. Fasting from "curated applause"—abstaining from social-media engagement that seeks likes and shares—functions as a modern fast, resisting the furnace of digital idolatries. Participants might deactivate notifications for a week or refrain from posting achievements online, redirecting time toward private prayer and communal service. Embodied liturgies also include wearing simple symbols—unbranded clothing or minimalistic accessories—that reject consumerist idolatries. Groups can coordinate "liturgical flash mobs"—gatherings where participants pray silently or sing worship songs in public venues frequented by commercial advertising—creating witness to alternative allegiances. Such practices refabricate public spaces as arenas of sacred witness rather than marketplaces of desire. By integrating body, environment, and ritual, these embodied liturgies root defiant worship in everyday contexts.

5.5.3 Forming "Furnace Circles" for Mutual Intercession and Accountability

Just as the three Hebrews endured the furnace together, modern believers benefit from forming small, confidential circles dedicated to mutual support under pressure. "Furnace circles" meet regularly—weekly or biweekly—to share upcoming challenges where cultural pressures threaten conscience, then intercede specifically for one another. Each member brings a personal "furnace prayer request," whether it involves a corporate policy conflict, family opposition to faith, or anticipated legal challenges. The group practices listening without judgment, offering spiritual and practical counsel grounded in Scripture. Accountability agreements outline confidentiality norms, attendance expectations, and reciprocal commitments to pray and provide resources. Circles might use shared digital platforms to update prayer needs, report answered prayers, and coordinate advocacy efforts. Periodic residential retreats strengthen bonds, combine spiritual disciplines, and simulate furnace scenarios through role-playing, preparing members for actual tests. Leaders rotate facilitation to cultivate mutual ownership and prevent dependency on a single mentor. These circles function as early-warning systems, spotting subtle shifts toward compromise and intervening with restorative practices. Furnace circles thus institutionalize solidarity, ensuring that no believer faces trials alone.

5.5.4 Crafting Public Statements that Combine Truth-Telling with Neighbor Love

Defiant worship often requires articulating convictions in public forums—op-eds, social-media posts, speeches—where rhetoric can easily polarize. Learning from Daniel's blend of candor and respect, believers craft statements that state biblical truths clearly while expressing empathy for those who hold opposing views. Such statements open by affirming shared values—human dignity, common good—before explaining why certain practices violate covenantal norms. Language is chosen to avoid contempt; instead, it invites dialogue and welcomes questions. Public declarations can be prayerful, concluding with an invitation to join in prayer rather than issuing ultimatums. When read at public meetings or posted online, these statements model defiant worship that does not dehumanize opponents. Feedback loops—sharing drafts with furnace circles or trusted mentors—help refine tone and content. Platforms might include joint declarations across denominations and ideologies, amplifying collective witness. By combining truth-telling with neighbor love, these public statements reflect the gospel's dual commitments to justice and mercy. They demonstrate that obedience to God's word need not abandon compassion, embodying the character of King Jehoshaphat's decree to seek the Lord with all their heart (2 Chronicles 20:12).

5.6 Writing on the Wall: Calling a Culture to Account

5.6.1 From Furnace Vindication to Banquet Judgment in Belshazzar's Hall

The dramatic reversal from furnace deliverance to banquet condemnation illustrates how God's favor toward faithful witnesses serves as a precursor to broader cultural reckoning. After Hananiah, Mishael, and Azariah emerged unscathed from the flames, Darius issued a decree acknowledging "no other god can save like this" (Daniel 3:29), opening a brief window of imperial humility. Yet the same empire soon relapsed into decadence under Belshazzar, whose blasphemous feast desecrated sacred vessels and ignored divine warnings. This pendulum swing underscores that grace extended to individuals does not guarantee lasting institutional repentance;

cultures may receive mercy yet revert to self-exaltation. Belshazzar's banquet scene, fraught with drunken revelry and sacrilege, contrasts sharply with the sober worship of the furnace three, revealing how proximity to religious truth without repentance leads to greater guilt. The sudden appearance of the disembodied hand writing on the wall dramatizes God's audit of unrepentant societies, pronouncing "MENE, TEKEL, PARSIN" as an indictment of "numbered," "weighed," and "divided" governance (Daniel 5:25–28). The trajectory from furnace vindication to banquet judgment warns readers that personal faithfulness may postpone but does not obviate cultural accountability. It foreshadows the necessity for ongoing prophetic critique, even after victories of deliverance. This narrative movement invites reflection on how current societies, having glimpsed the power of devout witness, might still cycle back into systemic sin without sustained repentance. It also prepares readers to recognize the writing on their own cultural walls—signs that judgment looms if justice and mercy remain unheeded. As we transition to Belshazzar's feast, we will unpack the dynamics of sacrilege, divine communication, and the urgency of cultural critique rooted in covenant faithfulness.

5.6.2 Previewing Prophetic Confrontation with Societal Decadence

The Belshazzar episode exemplifies the moment when unquestioned privilege meets uncompromising divine standards, triggering a prophetic confrontation that spares neither palace nor populace. Prophets throughout Scripture—Jeremiah in Jerusalem, Ezekiel by the Kebar, Amos on Bethel's altars—echo this pattern of calling out cultural depravity from within social centers of power. In Belshazzar's hall, revelers trampled sacred boundaries by drinking from temple vessels while praising deities of gold and silver (Daniel 5:3). The divine response—an inscrutable handwriting on the wall—bypassed human reasoning and shattered royal complacency in a single moment. This scene models how God speaks to societies in ways that disrupt mundane celebrations, demanding immediate moral clarity. Upcoming analysis will explore how prophets employ symbol, sign-act, and direct speech to confront societal sin, inviting both leaders and citizens into repentance. We will examine the theological implications of God's judgment as both corrective and covenantal, aimed at restoration rather than mere destruction. Drawing parallels to modern contexts—rampant consumer waste, political corruption, cultural coarsening—we will discern how prophetic critique remains essential for any community flirting with self-worship. The contrast between furnace deliverance and banquet doom sets up a broader theme: that individual and communal faith must deepen into courageous cultural engagement, lest divine patience be mistaken for permission. As we delve into Daniel 5, readers will encounter strategies for prophetic dialogue that honor truth, balance mercy, and call societies to accountable transformation.

5.6.3 Invitation to Identify Personal "Fiery Furnaces" and Rehearse Trust

Before entering the banquet hall of Belshazzar's decadence, readers are challenged to locate their own "furnace" moments—situations where standing for covenant loyalty exacts real cost. These modern furnaces may appear as demands for compromise in workplace ethics, pressures to conform on social media, or calls to abandon convictions in public forums. The invitation is to rehearse trust by engaging small-scale furnaces first: perhaps standing for truth in a team meeting, refusing ethically dubious assignments, or upholding justice when it is unpopular. Rehearsal builds spiritual muscle, ensuring that when higher-stakes tests arise, the heart instinctively turns to Yahweh rather than expedient alliances. This preparatory step involves identifying potential flashpoints, gathering "furnace circles" of prayerful allies, and practicing disciplines—fasting, public confession, or symbolic acts of solidarity—that mirror the Hebrews' experience. Participants might script personal declarations of faith to recite when pressured or create contingency plans for legal and relational fallout. By simulating these trials in low-stakes environments, communities incubate courage and clarity for future reckonings. This process roots Luke 5:25's promise in lived experience: "The one who calls you is faithful, and he will do it." Such intentional preparation positions believers not merely as observers of Belshazzar's downfall but as active participants in the ongoing drama of divine justice and mercy. As we move into Chapter 6, readers will be equipped to recognize the writing on their own walls and respond with covenantal confidence.

Conclusion

The furnace narrative illuminates a timeless paradox: the fire that threatens to destroy the faithful often becomes the venue of their deepest communion with God. Hananiah, Mishael, and Azariah modeled nonviolent defiance that did not seek conflict but refused complicity, turning state-sanctioned ritual into an opportunity for worship. Their solidarity broke the empire's will to enforce uniform conformity, and their miraculous vindication reshaped imperial policy, granting protections for conscience that echoed far beyond Babylon's borders. Their legacy compels contemporary believers to recognize the "golden images" of our age—be they nationalist fervor, consumer culture, or enforced ideologies—and to prepare for "fires" of testing with disciplines of mutual intercession, liturgical creativity, and prophetic clarity. In every furnace of pressure, the same promise holds true: when we stand unwavering, God's presence walks with us, and He alone emerges unscathed.

Chapter 6 – Warning a Decadent Culture: Belshazzar and the Writing on the Wall

On the night that Babylon's walls were thought impregnable, a revel of imperial arrogance morphed into a scene of divine confrontation. Belshazzar's feast, lavish beyond measure and sacrilegious in its appropriation of holy vessels, crystallized a culture that had forgotten its founding covenant and embraced power as its ultimate god. In that moment of unchecked luxury and denial, the silent hand of heaven traced an unignorable verdict, halting the revelers in their tracks. This chapter explores how the writing on the wall served as both an indictment of systemic hubris and a clarion call to collective repentance. Through historical investigation, theological reflection, and contemporary parallels, we will uncover what it means for any society to be "weighed and found wanting," and how God's judgments can open the way for genuine renewal.

6.0 Banquet on the Brink—Framing the Fall of an Empire

6.0.1 From Nebuchadnezzar's Reforms to Belshazzar's Regression

Nebuchadnezzar's reign showcased the tension between divine humility and imperial pride, illustrated when he acknowledged Yahweh's sovereignty after a period of madness (Daniel 4:34–37). His public confession signaled that true power comes not from might but from reverent submission. Yet his successors, lacking his spiritual conviction, drifted into self-aggrandizement. Belshazzar, his grandson or co-regent depending on sources, inherited a palace lavishly built and a bureaucracy steeped in conquest. The absence of Daniel's guiding presence in court marked a void soon filled by flatterers and astrologers. Where Nebuchadnezzar had welcomed prophetic critique, Belshazzar dismissed any memory of divine intervention, choosing instead to indulge his own appetites. The golden image that later stood on the Dura plain represented a full regression from Nebuchadnezzar's later humility back to unchecked imperial self-worship. Babylon's transition from humbled servant to defiant tyrant spanned just one generation, demonstrating how quickly spiritual gains can be lost. The heart of the empire reverted to valuing spectacle over substance, ceremony over covenant, mirroring many modern institutions that forget foundational principles once immediate threats recede. This generational drift warns readers that preserving faithfulness in leadership demands constant renewal, lest complacency and comfort erode moral vigilance. Understanding this trajectory illuminates why the banquet that crowns Belshazzar's reign becomes the stage for divine intervention.

6.0.2 Feasting inside a Besieged City—Denial as a Coping Mechanism

By 539 BC, Babylon lay under siege by the combined forces of Media and Persia, its walls thought impregnable yet secretly undermined. Despite the looming threat, Belshazzar ordered a grand feast, inviting dignitaries and officials to rejoice under false security. The banquet became a psychological refuge from external danger, masking anxiety with wine, music, and revelry. Such denial through indulgence parallels modern tendencies to distract ourselves with entertainment when crises loom—whether financial markets wobble or environmental warnings escalate. The court musicians played layered melodies to drown out whispers of doom, while revelers toasted pagan deities in a desperate attempt to secure their fates. Their behavior reveals how moments of national peril can precipitate collective denial, substituting festivity for foresight. The consumption of luxury goods amid scarcity highlighted the elite's detachment from civilian suffering, undermining social cohesion. Wealthy courtiers indulged in exotic delicacies while the populace endured siege conditions, escalating social resentment that often precedes systemic collapse. Rather than addressing structural weaknesses, leaders doubled down on spectacle, illustrating how denial can become state policy. This pattern resonates in contemporary contexts where political and corporate leaders sponsor opulent events even as broader constituencies grapple with austerity or climate crises. Recognizing denial's function as a coping mechanism equips readers to discern when comfort rituals obscure underlying decay and to advocate for transparency rather than distraction.

6.0.3 Daniel's Decades-Long Silence and the Emergency Summons

During Nebuchadnezzar and Darius's reigns, Daniel served faithfully, interpreting dreams and advising kings, yet his voice recedes in the Babylonian narrative until the writing appears on the wall. His prolonged silence in court intrigues may reflect respect for political processes or a disciplined restraint, waiting only for moments of divine imperative. When Belshazzar desecrated temple vessels and blasphemed the God of Israel, the king's attendants immediately summoned Daniel as a last resort. The abrupt summons—from celebration to crisis—underscores that prophetic intervention follows human exhaustion of all other options. This dynamic mirrors Jesus' rebuke of the Pharisees, "You hypocrites! You can discern the face of the sky but cannot discern the signs of the times" (Matthew 16:3). Daniel's emergence from relative courtly obscurity into a moment of existential drama exemplifies how faithful observers become essential witnesses when cultures cross critical moral thresholds. His readiness—fueled by decades of disciplined devotion—enabled him to speak truth under pressure without hesitation. This pattern teaches modern readers that sustained faithfulness, even when unrecognized, prepares individuals for pivotal moments of societal reckoning. Daniel's career thus models how quiet diligence lays the groundwork for urgent prophetic action when moral collapse accelerates.

6.0.4 When Conscience Is Ignored, God Interrupts Comfort with Confrontation

The revelry of Belshazzar's feast, unchecked by ethical self-examination, provoked God's dramatic intrusion—the appearance of a disembodied hand. This supernatural interruption illustrates that divine patience has limits and that moral complacency triggers corrective judgment. The hand's writing halted the instruments and froze the participants, externalizing an internal failure of conscience. By inscribing messages on palace plaster, God made visible the hidden guilt that festivities and denial had attempted to muffle. This event parallels prophetic illustrations in Amos 5:21–24, where God rejects empty songs and festivals when justice is absent. The sudden confrontation shocks both rulers and guests into a realization that earthly comfort cannot substitute for covenantal fidelity. In contemporary terms, cultural reckonings—economic crashes, social upheavals, environmental disasters—function as similar divine "writings," demanding accountability. When societies ignore warning signs—rising inequality, systemic injustice, sacrilegious appropriation of sacred symbols—crises emerge to force reflection. The furnace deliverance of Daniel's friends offered mercy within judgment, but Belshazzar's feast reveals that repeated desecration invites harsher consequences. This pattern calls modern believers to proactively heed conscience's whispers rather than wait for looming catastrophes to drive repentance. Understanding the interplay between comfort and confrontation prepares readers for the detailed study of the writing on the wall that follows.

6.1 The Last Night of Babylon (539 BC)

6.1.1 Geo-Political Fault Lines

By the late sixth century BC, the Babylonian Empire faced a coalition of Medes and Persians who skillfully exploited vulnerabilities in the city's defenses. Persian prince Cyrus gathered forces along the southern frontier while Media's army pressured from the north. Intelligence networks in the provinces eroded loyalty to Belshazzar as civic officials hedged bets on a new regime. Babylon's famed walls—despite boasting widths of 25 feet—belied weaknesses in their foundations, exploited by diverting the Euphrates River. Engineers dug channels to lower water levels, enabling troops to march beneath the gates undetected. Babylon's governors, intoxicated by near-century of unchallenged supremacy, ignored these strategic shifts. Biblical narratives often highlight how God overturns mighty fortresses by unconventional means, recalling Gideon's mid-battle lamp and trumpet tactics (Judges 7). The geopolitical storm gathering around Babylon parallels contemporary shifts in global power balances, where technological innovation and alliance flux can topple even the most entrenched hegemonies. Recognizing fault lines demands sober analysis, community wisdom, and willingness to heed early warnings—values Daniel embodied in his century-long counsel to rulers.

6.1.2 Royal Hubris and Historical Amnesia

Belshazzar's co-regency under his absentee father Nabonidus left him insecure on the throne, prompting exaggerated displays of authority. Insisting on leading the feast himself, he displayed temple vessels, hailing them as trophies of conquest. This public flaunting of sacred objects demonstrated cultural amnesia, erasing Nebuchadnezzar's later spiritual transformation. By ignoring his grandfather's testimony before the gathered masses, Belshazzar denied the very legacy that could have tempered his arrogance. Historical records show that royal inscriptions omitted any acknowledgments of past humiliation, preferring tales of unbroken triumph. This purposeful forgetting cultivated a court culture averse to self-critique, where flattery trumped honesty. The Hebrew prophets repeatedly warned against such amnesia: "Remember the days of old; consider the years of many generations" (Deuteronomy 32:7). Belshazzar's hubris, fed by selective memory, blinded him to the cyclical nature of empires and the moral debts incurred by desecration. Modern leaders can similarly fall prey to historical amnesia when organizational successes eclipse lessons learned from past errors, reinforcing the need for institutional remembrance.

6.1.3 Desecration of Sacred Vessels

The temple in Jerusalem housed vessels dedicated to Yahweh's service—gold and silver cups, bowls, and utensils used in sacrificial rites. During Babylon's earlier conquest, Nebuchadnezzar had seized these objects and stored them in the temple of his god Bel at Babylon (Daniel 5:2). Belshazzar's decision to retrieve and use these vessels for secular drinking demonstrated contempt for the holiness they symbolized. Each sip from these cups represented a profane act against a covenant people and their God. The bowls, once vessels of sacrament, became drinking goblets praising Babylonian deities. This repurposing of sacred objects echoes Jesus' lament over Pharisaic misuse of the temple, where external rites covered internal corruption (Matthew 23:27). By blurring the boundary between sacred and secular, Belshazzar's feast inverted the divine order, foreshadowing divine judgment. Desecration accelerated the moral decay of the empire, signaling that no aspect of national life remained untouched by idolatry. This act demands contemporary reflection on how we treat symbols of faith—whether churches market their spaces for profit or believers trivialize holy rituals for entertainment. Understanding the gravity of such desecration equips communities to guard sacred boundaries and treat religious symbols with reverence.

6.1.4 Liturgical Mockery and Collective Numbness

As guests sang to "gods of gold and silver, bronze and iron, wood and stone" (Daniel 5:4), the palace choir functioned like a liturgical engine driving mass desensitization. Each repetition of the ritualized toasts eroded participants' capacity to feel moral qualms, numbing their consciences under a deluge of communal affirmation. Musical accompaniments—drumbeats, lyres, flutes—transformed dissent into dissonance that no one was willing to voice. This orchestration of liturgical mockery reflects Paul's warning against "exchanging the truth about God for a lie" (Romans 1:25), showing how communal rituals can invert right worship into collective idolatry. The spectacle stimulated dopamine loops in the brain akin to modern entertainment, creating addictive patterns that stifle critical reflection. Mass participation in such liturgies becomes a form of voluntary servitude, where individuals forego personal convictions for group identity. Daniel, called to interpret this scene, had to pierce through layers of spectacle to remind the king that true worship belongs to Yahweh alone. Contemporary societies face similar risks through mass media events and viral challenges that confer belonging at the expense of truth. Recognizing liturgical mockery prepares readers to reclaim authentic communal worship as a countercultural act of conscience.

6.2 Mene, Tekel, Parsin—The Divine Audit

6.2.1 The Hand That Halts the Party

In the midst of uproarious celebration, a disembodied hand materialized and scrawled words on the palace wall, creating a tableau of supernatural interruption. This sudden silence exemplifies God's prerogative to override human agendas, transforming merriment into sober reckoning. The hand's visibility made literal what conscience had long whispered: that injustice and sacrilege carry consequences. Unlike prophets who spoke from mouths of flesh, this divine handwriting needed no intermediary, underscoring the immediacy of judgment. The Babylonian scribes who examined the script could not decipher its meaning, highlighting the limitations of human wisdom apart from divine revelation. This motif recurs in Revelation 2–3, where letters to churches convey direct messages from Christ, interrupted only by pursuit of repentance. The hand's image remains a powerful reminder that, when all human devices fail, God writes directly on hearts and walls to call for accountability.

6.2.2 Weighed and Found Wanting—Theology of Judgment

The terms "Mene, Tekel, Parsin" translate respectively as "numbered," "weighed," and "divided." "Mene" declares that Belshazzar's days were numbered, echoing the Hebrew concept of God measuring out human lifespans (Psalm 139:16). "Tekel" proclaims that he was weighed on divine scales and found deficient, referencing the prophetic critique of dishonest balances in Amos 8:5. "Parsin" signals division of his kingdom, foreshadowing its immediate conquest by Medes and Persians. This triad encapsulates a covenantal metric: God measures nations by justice, weighs leaders by integrity, and divides empires that reject divine standards. It reframes judgment not as arbitrary vengeance but as the inexorable outcome of moral failure. Daniel's translation exposes the theological backbone of the writing, reminding contemporary readers that cultures are accountable to a transcendent ethics that transcends political ideologies. His interpretation aligns with Proverbs' admonition that "the Lord weighs the hearts" (Proverbs 21:2), signaling that hidden motives never escape divine scrutiny.

6.2.3 Daniel's Fearless Prophetic Voice

Despite his advanced age and the volatile atmosphere, Daniel entered the banquet hall unhesitatingly to interpret the inscription. He addressed the king with respectful candor, refusing to flatter Belshazzar or mince words. By linking the writing to divine audit metrics, Daniel exposed the king's moral failures without personal attack, focusing on covenant unfaithfulness rather than individual character. His prophetic voice carried the authority not of human office but of God's messenger, reminiscent of Elijah's confrontations with Ahab (1 Kings 18) and Jeremiah's rebukes of Judah's leaders (Jeremiah 1). Daniel's boldness reflected decades of disciplined devotion, cultivated in prayer-silences and dream interpretations. His choice to speak truth in the face of immediate danger modeled prophetic courage for all who serve society's highest offices. This moment underscores that faithfulness sometimes demands risking comfort and even life itself to uphold divine justice.

6.2.4 A Sentence Carried Out Before Dawn

No sooner had Daniel finished interpreting the writing than the Medo-Persian forces gained entry to Babylon by night, emptying the city without open battle (Herodotus 1.191). Belshazzar was slain, and Darius the Mede assumed control, fulfilling the ancient forecast of division and deposition. The swiftness of the conquest—executed under cover of darkness—mirrors the immediacy of God's verdict, showing that delayed repentance results in abrupt overthrow. Babylon's fall without protracted warfare emphasizes that divine judgment bypasses human defenses, undermining the illusion of invincibility. The transfer of power sealed the writing's meaning: nations blind to moral decay will find their supposed strength turned to dust when divine timing arrives. For Daniel, this upheaval confirmed that prophetic words carry both warning and certainty. Modern societies ignoring prophetic admonitions may likewise awaken to systemic collapse, underscoring the urgency of heeding divine audits before dawn breaks on unsuspecting kingdoms.

6.3 Diagnostic Lessons for Contemporary Societies

6.3.1 Hubris Revisited—The Perils of Nostalgic Grandeur

Modern nations frequently cling to past glories as if they guarantee future invincibility, echoing Belshazzar's blind pride in Babylon's unmatched heritage. Leaders trumpet historic victories and build monuments to national achievements, yet often neglect the societal rot that festers beneath triumphant retellings. Such nostalgia creates an intellectual syndrome where critical self-examination is replaced by mythic affirmation. Economies built on resource extraction or one-industry dominance face collapse when external conditions shift, yet cultural memory resists acknowledging new realities. The repetition of nationalist slogans and state-sponsored festivals functions like the golden statue on the Dura plain, demanding unquestioned loyalty to a past that no longer exists. Educational curricula that sanitize or romanticize history fail to prepare citizens for emerging challenges, fostering collective amnesia. In corporate contexts, companies that rest on brand legacy while ignoring market disruption find themselves overtaken by agile competitors. Scripture's repeated warnings—"Be not wise in your own eyes" (Proverbs 3:7)—invite humility by recalling that God raises up and brings down rulers (Daniel 2:21). Prophetic voices today must challenge nostalgic narratives that impede adaptive policies, urging citizens to learn from history rather than idolize it. Community dialogues grounded in truth-telling can test for historical blind spots and cultivate resilience for future uncertainties. By confronting hubris, communities reclaim the capacity to innovate responsibly, aligning national self-understanding with ethical sobriety. This leads naturally to examining structural injustice, the other weight on human scales.

6.3.2 Injustice—The Hidden Weight on Modern Scales

Just as the false balances in Belshazzar's kingdom provoked divine condemnation, contemporary societies harbor hidden injustices that weigh heavily on national integrity. Economic systems that exploit low-wage labor or perpetuate poverty create underclasses whose suffering remains invisible within affluent sectors. Injustice also manifests in mass incarceration, where policies disproportionately target marginalized communities, echoing repressive legalism used against three Hebrew youths. Modern banking practices—predatory lending, hidden fees—mirror false weights, profiting from vulnerability. Technology firms collect personal data without transparent consent, commodifying human dignity for corporate gain. Environmental neglect, too, imposes injustices on future generations who inherit degraded ecosystems, replicating sacrilege against creation (Genesis 2:15). Prophets like Amos condemned those who sold the righteous for silver and the needy for wine (Amos 2:6), a rhythm seen today when profit motives override social welfare. Addressing these injustices requires diagnostic clarity—mapping systems of privilege and oppression, then enacting reforms that recalibrate societal scales. Legal advocacy, policy audits, and restorative justice initiatives function as modern prophetic instruments, exposing and redressing harm. Faith communities can partner with secular organizations in poverty alleviation and criminal justice reform, embodying covenantal justice. Public education campaigns reveal hidden burdens, inviting collective responsibility rather than silent complicity. By rooting economic and legal structures in ethics of fairness, societies invite divine blessing rather than moral bankruptcy. These lessons on injustice segue into reflections on sacrilege—misuse of the sacred for profit or propaganda.

6.3.3 Sacrilege—When the Sacred Becomes a Selfie Prop

In Belshazzar's feast, temple vessels—holy instruments of worship—became party props, reflecting a profound misapplication of the sacred. Today's cultural equivalents include branding religious symbols for marketing or trivializing holy rituals for social-media clout. Churches that host consumer-oriented "faith festivals" risk reducing spiritually formative gatherings to entertainment spectacles. Tech companies gamify spiritual practices—prayer apps that award badges for streaks—turning devotion into a commodity. Sacred spaces rented for secular events further blur the line between reverence and irreverence. Such practices mirror the graffiti-like desecration on Babylon's walls, where what was consecrated transforms into a prop for worldly applause. The biblical injunction "you shall not profane my holy name" (Leviticus 22:2) warns that misuse of the sacred renders worship void of power. Modern communities must discern where reverence ends and spectacle begins, reestablishing boundaries that honor holiness rather than co-opt it for convenience. Liturgical guidelines—setting aside consecrated time, spaces, and symbols exclusively for worship—reinforce this distinction. Educating congregations on the history and theology of sacred objects counters casual appropriation. When sacred music is repackaged as background for advertisements, believers can advocate for content integrity. Spiritual directors can teach practitioners to approach rituals with attentiveness rather than performance mindset. These measures restore the sacred's dignity and prepare societies to receive prophetic critique and engage civically.

6.3.4 Prophetic Critique and Civic Engagement Today

Daniel's fearless admonitions to Babylonian kings exemplify the synergy of prophetic critique and practical governance. Modern believers can follow his lead by translating theological insights into policy actions that address injustice, structural sin, and sacrilege. Prophetic critique begins with moral diagnosis—identifying where cultural practices conflict with covenant values—then moves to public witness: op-eds, legislative testimonies, and community forums. Civic engagement tools include impact assessments that measure policies against biblical ethics: does a criminal-justice reform bill advance dignity and redemption? Do environmental regulations honor creation care? Faith-based coalitions can commission social-impact audits for corporate and governmental entities, offering recommendations grounded in justice and mercy. Petition campaigns and peaceful demonstrations embody non-violent resistance to unethical laws, modeled on Hananiah et al.'s civil disobedience. Simultaneously, alliances with secular advocacy groups ensure broad support and minimize sectarian polarities. Prophetic voices must also propose constructive alternatives—voting reforms, economic redistribution models, transparent data-privacy frameworks. Public theology conferences provide platforms for dialogue between clergy, policymakers, and civic leaders. Through such integrated engagement, faith communities can steer societies toward alignment with divine justice rather than mere cultural trends. These approaches set the stage for recovering hope after divine audits, showing that judgment can yield renewal rather than despair.

6.3.5 Hope after the Handwriting

Despite the severity of the "Mene, Tekel, Parsin" verdict, Scripture underscores that divine judgment often precedes restoration. Cyrus's decree permitting exiles to return and rebuild Jerusalem's temple (Ezra 1:1–4) illustrates how God can transform judgment into opportunity for renewal. Likewise, modern reforms—legislation to protect religious liberties, economic stimulus after crises, truth commissions after conflict—embody hope that societies heed divine corrections. The pattern of fall and restoration invites communities to view current reckonings as callings to rebuild structures on firmer ethical foundations. Grassroots movements promoting reconciliation and restorative justice reflect this redemptive arc. Hope also emerges through spiritual renewal—revival services, community repentance gatherings, and interdenominational prayers for national healing. Art, literature, and music inspired by themes of judgment and mercy can foster collective resilience, reinforcing belief that no moral collapse is beyond God's restorative power. A theology of hope acknowledges pain and loss but affirms that divine sovereignty over history ensures that fidelity to God yields enduring transformation. This hopeful posture bridges the act of critique with proactive construction, inviting societies to participate in God's redemptive economy rather than resigning to doom. As we turn to practices for forming prophetic discernment communities, this hope provides the motivation and framework for sustained engagement.

6.4 Forming Prophetic Communities—Practices for Cultural Discernment

6.4.1 Fixed-Hour Prayer for National Leaders and Marginalized Neighbors

Adopting Daniel's thrice-daily prayer rhythm as a corporate practice can shape prophetic communities attuned to national needs and minority voices. Designated prayer hours—morning, midday, evening—create intentional pauses to intercede for policymakers, shrinking cultural echo chambers. Participants might pray for specific issues—justice reforms, environmental stewardship, refugee rights—rooting petitions in scriptural petitions for the foreigner (Deuteronomy 10:18–19). In office buildings, quiet prayer corners can host cross-sector intercessors who receive real-time policy updates and respond with prayerful discernment. Online platforms enable national prayer networks to synchronize, linking rural and urban believers in unified petitions. Prayer texts drawn from Lamentations or Psalm 85 guide confession of collective sins and pleas for restoration. Prayer circles can invite stories from marginalized communities, amplifying their needs in corporate intercession. Over time, these rhythms cultivate a prophetic sensitivity to "cries of the city," aligning communal worship with

God's heart for the oppressed. This practice transitions naturally into historical journaling, preserving insights for successive generations.

6.4.2 Historical Journaling: Tracking Societal "Warning Signs" alongside Scripture

Prophetic communities benefit from systematic journaling that logs observed cultural "warnings"—policy failures, ethical breaches, sacrilegious events—alongside corresponding biblical passages. This practice functions like spiritual analytics, revealing patterns of hubris, injustice, or idolatry over time. Journals may include news clips, personal reflections, and prayers, creating an archive for group reflection and teaching. Quarterly review sessions compare journal entries with scriptural prophetic texts—Amos's oracles against Israel's injustices or Jeremiah's laments over Judah's covenant breaches. Such reflection fosters communal discernment, preventing isolated interpretations and confirming recurring themes. Journals become teaching tools for raising new prophetic voices, ensuring that lessons learned inform future engagement. Digital tools—shared online documents or specialized apps—enable geographically dispersed communities to collaborate seamlessly. This discipline reinforces that prophetic clarity arises not solely from spontaneous insight but also from sustained observation and scriptural correlation. As communities sharpen their vision through journaling, artistic protest emerges as a complementary modality.

6.4.3 Artistic Protest: Murals, Spoken-Word, and Digital Design Echoing "Mene, Tekel" Themes

Artistic protest channels prophetic critique into public spaces through creative media that engage hearts more deeply than polemics alone. Murals depicting broken scales or fading national symbols can remind passersby of hidden injustices. Spoken-word performances in community centers dramatize the tension between cultural self-exaltation and divine accountability, inviting emotional resonance. Digital designers create shareable graphics—social-media posters featuring "Weighed and Found Wanting" captions—sparking online conversations. Collaborative art projects, such as mosaic installations made with donated temple vessel replicas, evoke the desecration of sacred time and call viewers to repentance.

Workshops train participants to translate journaled insights into visual or performative expressions, equipping laypeople as prophetic artists. Partnerships with local theaters and galleries integrate these works into civic festivals, challenging cultural complacency. By embedding art in daily life—covering bus stops, community boards, and public parks—prophetic messages reach broader audiences than traditional sermons. Artistic protest transforms empty spaces into stages for divine encounters, bridging critique and hope. These initiatives lead naturally into hospitality tables that model countercultural feasting under covenant values.

6.4.4 Hospitality Tables that Redeem Belshazzar's Banquet— Honoring the Sacred, Feeding the Poor

Countering the desecration of temple vessels at Belshazzar's feast, prophetic communities can host "hospitality tables" that sanctify shared meals with sacramental intention. These events reclaim feasting as an act of covenantal unity rather than imperial spectacle. Simple tablecloths and unadorned cups symbolize humility, while readings from Isaiah 25:6–9 remind participants of God's vision for a banquet where tears are wiped away. Guests include marginalized neighbors—refugees, homeless individuals, survivors of injustice—ensuring that hospitality tables embody biblical care for the least (Matthew 25:35–36). Facilitators open with prayers of confession for cultural sacrilege and petitions for systemic renewal. During the meal, leaders share journaled "warning signs" and collective prayers, fostering embodied liturgies that integrate critique with compassion. Post-meal discussions explore structural injustices and propose tangible advocacy steps. By linking communal feasting with prophetic reflection, hospitality tables transform public spaces into sanctuaries of memory and hope. These practices cultivate solidarity, ensuring that prophetic communities remain grounded in tangible expressions of mercy and justice.

6.5 Faithfulness in the Lion's Den

6.5.1 Daniel's Credibility Post-Belshazzar Sets Up Confrontation with New Bureaucratic Envy

The successful prophetic intervention in Belshazzar's hall significantly elevated Daniel's standing in the new Medo-Persian administration, yet this increase in influence also sparked resentment among native officials. His reputation for divine insight made him indispensable for statecraft, but it also rendered him a target for jealousy akin to the court intrigue that later led to the lions' den episode. Daniel's prominence thus illustrates the paradox of prophetic favor: divine endorsement can open doors but also inflame human envy. Contemporary leaders who courageously critique societal wrongs may similarly find their credibility used as evidence to provoke institutional backlash. Understanding Daniel's navigation of post-crisis politics equips modern believers to anticipate and mitigate envy-driven attacks. This anticipation transitions us from public prophesy to personal persecution, tracing how faithfulness under fire prepares for the next test in the lions' den.

6.5.2 Moving from Public Indictment to Personal Persecution

While delivering communal warnings carries broad impact, it often leads to personal consequences when empires resist accountability. Daniel's fearless admonitions to Belshazzar and subsequent favor under Darius set the stage for policies targeting his private devotion—namely, a law banning prayer to any deity except the king. This shift from addressing public sin to enforcing private conformity underscores how regimes silent on collective injustices may still quash individual faithfulness. Modern analogues appear when whistleblowers or faith-based employees face punitive measures for private convictions. Recognizing this pattern, readers can prepare by strengthening personal devotional rhythms and building supportive networks before confronting institutional demands. Daniel's transition from public prophetic role to personal test reveals the continuity of faithfulness in every context, whether on a grand stage or behind closed doors.

6.5.3 Invitation to Identify God's Handwriting in Our Institutions

Before stepping into their own lions' dens—situations demanding fidelity at personal cost—readers are called to discern the divine "writing on the wall" within their organizations and cultures. This involves listening for silenced voices, scanning for patterns of hubris or injustice, and discerning when corporate or civic policies desecrate sacred boundaries. By applying diagnostic tools—journal entries, communal discernment practices, and prophetic art—believers can detect early warning signs of moral decay. This proactive identification makes the path of defiance less reactive and more strategic, allowing faith communities to offer timely critique rather than emergency protests. Armed with such awareness, readers can align their private devotions, communal solidarity, and public witness for the trials ahead. As Chapter 7 unfolds, they will see how Daniel's unbroken prayer life equipped him to face the literal lions' den with unwavering trust in God's sovereignty.

Conclusion

Belshazzar's fall illustrates that no empire—ancient or modern—escapes the moral laws written by its Creator. The abrupt shift from pomp to judgment reminds us that when prosperity dulls conscience, divine disruption is inevitable. Yet even this drastic audit carries a hope: judgment paves the path for restoration when societies heed the call to justice, humility, and authentic worship. As we step away from Babylon's final night, the challenge remains clear: to recognize the "writing" in our own culture's echo chambers and to respond with a prophetic blend of truth, compassion, and actionable repentance. In doing so, we participate in the ongoing story of God's mercy that follows every warning he issues.

Chapter 7 – Faithfulness in the Lion's Den: Perseverance amid Systemic Opposition

When a society enshrines conformity and punishes dissent, even the most private acts of devotion become battlegrounds for integrity. Daniel's final trial under the Medo-Persian regime shows how unwavering fidelity to prayer, in the face of laws weaponized against conscience, transforms repression into a stage for divine rescue. His decision to maintain visible rhythms of intercession upended bureaucratic schemes and exposed the fragility of human authority. Through this episode we explore how systemic opposition operates—how envy masquerades as procedure, how legal frameworks can stifle faith, and how courage emerges not from rash rebellion but from disciplined consistency. By tracing Daniel's journey from decree to deliverance, we uncover principles for sustaining spiritual convictions in any institution that seeks to silence them.

7.0 Behind Palace Walls—Why Integrity Provokes Bureaucratic Backlash

Daniel's rapid rise in the newly conquered Medo-Persian administration disrupted settled power dynamics in the court. His promotion grounded in proven competence and prophetic insight threatened career satraps accustomed to seniority-based advancement. As one of the few foreigners granted trust by both Darius and Cyrus, Daniel embodied innovation that bypassed traditional channels, sparking envy among established officials. Bureaucracies often reward conformity over conviction, so Daniel's visible piety—open prayer facing Jerusalem—became a convenient target for those eager to curtail his influence. Transparency about his devotional rhythms left rivals with only one recourse: legislative sabotage. When institutions valorize uniformity, any form of distinctiveness can seem disloyal, especially when it comes with demonstrated excellence. Daniel's integrity, honed over decades of devotion (Daniel 6:10), made him a living critique of colleagues whose moral compromises disguised themselves as protocol. The story illustrates a universal principle: those who anchor decisions in transcendent values inevitably provoke resistance from peers whose security depends on human approval. Such resistance surfaces as "ethics" investigations or policy proposals that nominally apply to all but target one individual, reflecting zero-sum politics. In Daniel's era, the royal decree banning prayer for thirty days outwardly appeared neutral but functioned as a weaponized policy to eliminate a distinguished advisor. Modern parallels include non-compete clauses, gag orders, or social-media policies that silence dissenting voices under the guise of organizational cohesion. Daniel's example shows that spiritual practices—especially those public and consistent—expose institutional hypocrisies that would rather subvert conscience than reform. Recognizing this dynamic empowers believers today to anticipate backlash when fidelity intersects with structural power. Daniel's unyielding devotion, far from rendering him irrelevant, pressed the system to reveal its deepest vulnerabilities, setting the stage for divine vindication.

7.1 Political Manipulation and Prayer Bans

7.1.1 Anatomy of Satrap Envy

Envy in hierarchical systems often masquerades as concern for procedural fairness, yet its true motive is preserving entrenched privilege. In Daniel's case, satraps and governors observed his influence with growing alarm, perceiving that each act of royal favor for Daniel diminished their own standing. They conspired to create performance reviews and "ethics reports" alleging that Daniel had acted in self-interest rather than imperial service. These documents, drafted to appear legitimate, cited minor procedural deviations as evidence of misconduct. The groupthink among administrators gave rise to a manufactured unanimity that pressured King Darius: if everyone agreed Daniel was disloyal, the king would have to remove him to maintain unity. This tactic mirrors modern corporate audits weaponized against star performers who threaten the status quo. By framing critique as a collective consensus, envious officials bypassed individual dissent, making Daniel's removal seem like a matter of state necessity rather than personal vendetta. The episode underscores how high integrity and visibility can fuel covert campaigns to neutralize principled actors. Recognizing these patterns—performance metrics manipulated to create false compliance—allows believers to prepare for similar tactics in contemporary institutions. The satraps' envy thus prefigures the next step: drafting a prayer ban that targeted Daniel's singular devotion.

7.1.2 Crafting a Royal Decree as a Legislative Trap

Under Perso-Median law, a royal decree sealed by the king's signet was irreversible—a fact the conspirators exploited to ensnare Daniel. They proposed a thirty-day statute forbidding any petition to any god or human except King Darius, knowing Daniel would refuse. The legality of the decree was impeccable, yet its motive was clearly malicious. This legislative trap parallels modern non-compete agreements and gag orders that legally bind individuals far beyond their intended scope. By cloaking the decree in declarations of loyalty and state security, the satraps manufactured broad support, making opposition appear treasonous. The conspirators held Darius's hand as he signed, insulating him from the moral import of the law's collision with conscience. In essence, they leveraged "rule of law" to suppress spiritual practice—an inversion of justice that Scripture condemns (Amos 5:24). The decree's ostensible purpose—to affirm loyalty—became its actual purpose: facilitating Daniel's downfall. Modern analogues include workplace codes of conduct or corporate policies that, when unexamined, serve as instruments of ideological conformity. Understanding this dynamic highlights the need for vigilance when institutions draft rules without moral scrutiny.

7.1.3 Unbroken Daily Rhythm of Prayer

Daniel's commitment to praying three times daily—even after the decree—embodies a "rule of prayer windows" visible to all who passed his upper-story window (Daniel 6:10). These deliberate pauses transformed prayer from a private discipline into an embodied protest. His posture of kneeling with windows open signaled that his devotion transcended any earthly mandate. The theologian Paul described such unceasing prayer as the spiritual oxygen of faith (1 Thessalonians 5:17), sustaining believers amid trials. Daniel's public prayer rhythm echoed Psalm 55:17, where the psalmist declares, "Evening, morning and noon I cry out in distress, and he hears my voice." This continuity of intercession demonstrated that ritual rhythm can anchor identity when institutions weaponize policy. The prayer windows thwarted rivals' hopes that Daniel would cave under pressure, revealing instead his unwavering allegiance to God. His example challenges contemporary readers to integrate visible devotion into their routines, resisting policies that aim to privatize or ban faith expression.

7.1.4 Resisting the Cycle of Fear

Confronted by a law threatening imprisonment or worse, Daniel faced internal temptations: to pray in secret, to negotiate with officials, or to dangle partial compliance. He recognized that each compromise would erode conscience and invite further demands. His determination to remain visible in prayer reaffirmed the prophetic principle that obedience to God outweighs fear of human judgment (Acts 5:29). This choice exemplifies a posture of courageous transparency: rather than hiding his faith, Daniel used his public devotion to confront the law's injustice. His example encourages modern believers to resist cycles of fear that push them toward silence or complicity. Strategic visibility—praying at scheduled times in shared workspaces or faith forums—creates accountability and deters secret retreat. By refusing to bargain with fear, Daniel preserved the integrity of his worship, setting a pattern for perseverance under systemic opposition.

7.2 Deliverance and Vindication

7.2.1 Into the Pit—A Night among Predators

After the king reluctantly consigned Daniel to the lions' den, the court sealed the cave with his signet ring, symbolizing irrevocable commitment to the decree (Daniel 6:17). The physical dangers he faced were severe: lions' dens were not sanitized arenas but natural caverns inhabited by wild beasts. Exposure risked suffocation, hypothermia, and infection—ailments as lethal as the predators themselves. Yet Daniel descended into this crucible with a prayerful heart, trusting that the God who closed the mouths of lions in earlier times (2 Kings 17:25–26) would act again. That night, angelic protection manifested, echoing the "Fourth Man" motif from the furnace episode (Daniel 3:25). The unearthly calm that settled over the den underscores Scripture's assurance that God shelters His faithful in the darkest places (Psalm 91:1–4). The narrative foreshadows New Testament assurances of divine accompaniment in tribulation (Matthew 28:20), illustrating that perilous isolation can become the arena for God's miraculous presence. The den's darkness amplified Daniel's solitude, yet liturgies of petition transformed it into a sanctuary of confession and intercession for the king and nation.

7.2.2 Dawn Recognition and Royal Repentance

At first light, King Darius hurried to the lions' den—his royal robes brushing the dust—as a prophet might rush to a reluctant pavilion. He called out anxiously, "Daniel, servant of the living God, has your God, whom you serve continually, been able to rescue you?" (Daniel 6:20). When Daniel answered, John Bunyan's Pilgrim's Progress came to mind: "He hath given me life to get out of the lion's mouth." Darius's immediate relief triggered a lament that resembled a psalm of contrition and thanksgiving. He composed a decree urging all people to fear Daniel's God, acknowledging divine sovereignty over human affairs. This royal confession parallels Psalm 57, where David, under enemy threat, declares God's mercy and deliverance. Darius's admission broke the paralysis of fear in his court, demonstrating how authentic repentance can cascade through leadership circles.

7.2.3 Public Proclamation of God's Greatness

King Darius issued a proclamation that spanned his empire, stating, "I make a decree that in every dominion of my kingdom men tremble and fear before the God of Daniel" (Daniel 6:26). The missive combined political authority with theological testimony, binding Cyrus's satrapies to a framework of reverence for Yahweh. This empire-wide decree functioned like Cyrus's later edict permitting exiles to return (Ezra 1), reinforcing the pattern that divine deliverance leads to legal protections for faith communities. Diplomatic ripple effects included enhanced status for Jewish exiles and increased interest among Gentile subjects in Daniel's God. The proclamation also regularized minority protections, foreshadowing modern human-rights charters. By embedding theological affirmation in civil law, Darius elevated Daniel's God to the pantheon of recognized deities, but with the unique claim of life-giving power.

7.2.4 The Aftermath—Institutional Memory of Miracle

The lions'-den deliverance reshaped Medo-Persian administrative culture, instilling respect for Daniel's faithfulness and skepticism toward policies that targeted conscience. Satraps who had conspired found themselves subject to the same decree they had used to ensnare him. Their reversal into the den itself illustrated Proverbs 26:27: "Whoever digs a pit will fall into it." Subsequently, palace protocols were updated to include conscience-protections for religious observance, a prototype for later Roman edicts under Constantine. Persian chronicles recorded Daniel's miracle alongside Cyrus's conquests, ensuring that the event remained part of the empire's collective memory. Jewish communities preserved the story in liturgical readings and synagogue cycles, cementing Daniel's legacy across generations. This institutional memory functioned to deter future plots against devout officials while encouraging others to maintain faithful witness.

7.3 Persevering under Institutional Hostility Today

7.3.1 Modern Prayer Bans and Conscience Clauses

In many workplaces, formal policies on "professional conduct" inadvertently become prayer bans when employees are discouraged from any visible religious expression. Human-resources manuals that prohibit "disruptive" personal views often fail to distinguish between harassment and simple devotion. Courts in various jurisdictions have wrestled with whether praying at one's desk constitutes a protected religious exercise or an unwelcome proselytizing effort. In public schools, some administrations have banned student-led prayers at sporting events while allowing secular announcements, illustrating uneven application of inclusion policies. Universities adopt speech codes that classify religious speech as "hate" if it conflicts with prevailing campus ideologies, effectively muzzling minority viewpoints. Corporate diversity trainings sometimes brand faith-based convictions as "bias," pressuring employees to suppress their beliefs. Yet conscience-protection laws—such as Title VII in the U.S. Civil Rights Act—mandate reasonable accommodations for religious practices unless they impose undue hardship (42 U.S.C. § 2000e–2). Small businesses and nonprofits must navigate these clauses carefully, balancing inclusivity with respect for conscience. Faith-based nonprofits often negotiate exemptions to healthcare mandates, illustrating how statutory conscience protections can safeguard vital services. Health-care workers invoke conscience clauses to refuse participation in procedures like abortion, highlighting real-world vocational stakes. Government chaplains leverage explicit accommodation rules to conduct worship in public institutions, modeling constructive engagement. Military policies now include controlled spaces and times for religious observance, acknowledging soldiers' spiritual needs. Tech companies have begun offering "quiet rooms" for prayer and meditation, recognizing that spiritual disciplines benefit well-being and productivity. Internationally, nations vary: some strongly protect religious expression at work, while others criminalize public prayer in mixed-faith settings. Nonprofit legal clinics provide pro bono representation to employees facing faith-based discrimination, building coalitions across religious lines. These modern prayer bans and conscience-clause debates mirror the lions'-den decree in their attempt to weaponize policy against private devotion. Learning from Daniel's example, believers today must know their legal rights, document discriminatory incidents, and seek accommodations in good faith. By engaging HR departments and legislators, faith communities can advocate for balanced policies that honor both workplace coherence and individual conscience.

7.3.2 Forming Gentle Yet Unyielding Conviction

True conviction combines steadfastness with humility, echoing 1 Peter 3:15's call to "always be prepared to give an answer... with gentleness and respect." Developing such conviction begins with grounding beliefs in Scripture and theological reflection rather than in reactive outrage. Small-group study sessions can explore case studies where faith and workplace norms clashed, equipping participants to articulate their positions clearly. Role-playing exercises help individuals practice respectful dialogue under pressure, sharpening both content and tone. Spiritual disciplines—fixed-hour prayer, daily Scripture meditation, and communal lament—anchor the heart so that public advocacy flows from worship, not from pride. Journaling personal experiences of marginalization fosters self-awareness of emotional triggers and idolatrous desires for approval. Accountability partners remind one another of the gospel's priority of love over victory, ensuring that zeal does not become harshness. Communities establish "conversation covenants" that set rules for tone, listening, and confidentiality in difficult discussions. Prayer triads support members facing particular workplace challenges, interceding and sharing empathy rather than simply offering solutions. Occasional "courage retreats" gather small cohorts to fast and pray in environments of quiet reflection, renewing resolve. Leaders model gentle tenacity by publicly acknowledging the legitimacy of institutional concerns while proposing principled alternatives. When negotiating accommodations—such as time for prayer or dress-code exceptions—believers present clear rationales tied to concrete practices and shared benefits, avoiding abstract theological jargon. This posture disarms hostility and invites collaborative problem-solving. Over time, communities develop a reputation for thoughtful, winsome advocacy that combines unyielding commitment to conscience with a gracious spirit. Such credibility opens doors for ongoing dialogue and reduces the likelihood of punitive reprisals. In this way, gentleness and firmness coalesce into a resilient conviction that shines amid systemic opposition.

7.3.3 Legal Literacy and Strategic Advocacy

Understanding the legal landscape is essential for effective defense of religious liberty in institutions. Lay leaders can partner with legal experts to host workshops on relevant statutes—religious accommodation provisions, anti-discrimination laws, and human-rights codes. These sessions cover essential topics like the right to reasonable accommodation under employment law, limits of free-speech protections, and distinctions between protected beliefs and conduct. Mock legal clinics allow participants to draft accommodation requests, legal complaints, or amicus briefs, demystifying procedural steps. Faith-based organizations often form interfaith coalitions to lobby legislators for conscience protections, demonstrating broad support beyond a single tradition. Strategic advocacy also involves building relationships with empathetic HR personnel, union representatives, and compliance officers who can champion faith inclusion internally. Social-media campaigns that tell personal stories of workplace challenges can mobilize public opinion and attract media attention, pressuring institutions to revise punitive policies. Engaging corporate boards and policymakers through written testimony and public hearings amplifies the prophetic voice. Litigation remains a last resort, but well-organized legal defenses clarify gray areas in policy and set judicial precedents. Regularly updated resource guides—available online—help employees assess when to seek legal counsel versus when to pursue internal resolution. By combining legal literacy with relational advocacy, faith communities transform adversarial disputes into opportunities for institutional reform and broader public awareness.

7.3.4 Vocational Excellence as Apologetics

Daniel's hallmark was doing his job so well that even his persecutors could not deny his competence (Daniel 6:3). In modern contexts, vocational excellence functions as a form of apologetics, demonstrating that faithfulness does not hinder performance but enhances it. Professionals commit to continuous learning—advanced certifications, cross-disciplinary seminars, and mentorship programs—to maintain peak relevance. Excellence includes ethical dimensions: transparent communication, fair treatment of colleagues, and rigorous adherence to quality standards. When faith-driven employees exceed expectations in project delivery, client satisfaction, or team leadership, they earn moral authority that disarms critics. Highlighting ethics alongside outcomes in performance reviews positions integrity as integral to success. Faith communities can develop "excellence cohorts" where professionals share best practices for integrating worship rhythms with workplace deliverables. Presentations at industry conferences on the positive impact of spiritual disciplines—such as mindfulness or sabbatical policies—educate broader audiences about the intersection of faith and work. By excelling in their crafts, believers build trust that opens doors for deeper conversations about motivations and convictions. This vocational witness echoes Jesus' teaching that good works attract others to glorify the Father (Matthew 5:16). Over time, patterns of excellence accumulate into a reputation that fortifies individual resilience and fosters institutional goodwill.

7.4 Disciplines that Fortify Lions'-Den Faith

7.4.1 Rule of Prayer Windows: Visible, Scheduled, and Community-Known

Implementing a public "Rule of Prayer Windows" involves selecting specific times—such as 8:00 AM, 12:00 PM, and 5:00 PM—during which believers pause for brief, corporate prayer in view of colleagues. Announcing these windows via email signatures, intranet postings, or desk-side reminders normalizes the practice. Over time, coworkers come to expect these rhythms, reframing them as part of daily operations rather than anomalies. The consistency of these pauses invests prayer with institutional legitimacy, countering policies that marginalize direct conversations with God. Participants may gather for two minutes of silent reflection or a three-minute guided prayer led by rotating volunteers. Including non-believing colleagues by inviting them to a moment of "deep pause" fosters interfaith solidarity and mutual respect for contemplative space. Digital tools—calendar invites, ambient chimes—signal each window, ensuring synchronicity. Debrief sessions weekly allow participants to share insights or corporate revelations received during prayer. Documenting answered prayers in a shared log encourages community confidence and collective trust in divine faithfulness. This visible rule both asserts the irrepressibility of devotion and shapes institutional culture to accommodate spiritual practices.

7.4.2 Scripture Memorization for Crisis Recall

Memorizing key passages—such as Psalm 23, Isaiah 40:31, or Daniel 6:10—equips believers to summon spiritual truths instantly when confronted with policy threats. Workplace memorization programs assign a verse of the month, encouraging small-group recitations and mnemonic games. Mobile-app reminders prompt random recall challenges, reinforcing memory through spaced repetition. Periodic "scripture sprints" gather colleagues for timed memory trials, fostering camaraderie and shared spiritual capital. In moments of crisis—sudden policy announcements or hostile meetings—immediate recall of trusted verses anchors the heart, mirroring Daniel's prompt return to prayer. Memorized Scripture may also be quietly displayed on nameplates or badges for visual reminders without imposing on others. Leaders embed verses in project kickoff meetings and performance reviews, subtly shaping narratives of confidence. Memorization shifts biblical truths from external guides to internalized companions, enabling fresh application under pressure.

7.4.3 Fasting from Institutional Favors: Countering Subtle Bribery with Voluntary Simplicity

Institutions often entice top performers with perks—bonuses, exclusive retreats, status amenities—that can subtly compromise conscience by fostering dependency on organizational grace. Emulating Daniel's refusal of imperial delicacies (Daniel 1:8), believers can fast from select favors: declining first-class upgrades, opting out of lavish client entertainment, or rejecting recognition ceremonies that blur the line between appreciation and idolization. Voluntary simplicity—choosing modest accommodations and transportation—signals that character, not comfort, grounds loyalty. Teams might institute "gift-fast" quarters, refraining from accepting non-essential tokens, and reallocating equivalent funds to charitable causes. Such practices disrupt pipelines of subtle bribery, reminding participants that service to God outranks service to any institution. In group settings, public declarations of simplicity challenge the default culture of consumption, opening dialogue about priorities and ethics. This shared fast cultivates solidarity among those resisting institutional entrapments, reinforcing a corporate identity centered on gospel values rather than perks.

7.4.4 Accountability Quads: Four-Person Peer Groups for Transparent Confession and Intercession

Forming accountability quads—groups of four peers—establishes a safe space for confessing struggles, reporting back on fears, and interceding specifically for institutional challenges. Quads meet weekly for structured check-ins: each member shares one success, one struggle, and one prayer request. Ground rules ensure confidentiality, non-judgment, and mutual support. Rotating facilitation builds shared leadership skills and prevents hierarchical dynamics. Quads maintain shared journals—digital or paper—that track prayer requests, answered prayers, and lessons learned over time. During periods of intense institutional scrutiny, quads ramp up meetings to bi-weekly or daily check-ins, adapting to emergent needs. They conduct periodic retreats—half-day or weekend—combining prayer, Scripture reflection, and strategic planning for confronting policy threats. Quads coordinate "prayer watches" around major organizational events, ensuring disciplined intercession before, during, and after potentially hostile encounters. By embedding these small groups into broader networks, believers create layered accountability structures that withstand systemic pressure.

7.5 Apocalyptic Vision and Hope beyond Empires

7.5.1 Daniel's Survival Paves the Way for Cosmic Visions

Having emerged from the lions' den, Daniel gains the credibility and spiritual momentum to receive apocalyptic revelations that compose the heart of chapters 7–12. His deliverance signals that God vindicates His prophets, empowering them to speak into larger cosmic dramas of empires and end-times. The shift from narrative biography to apocalyptic vision underscores that personal faithfulness precedes universal insight. Readers are thus invited to cultivate their own "lions'-den" fidelity—through prayer, disciplines, and communal support—so that they too might apprehend divine purposes beyond immediate crises.

7.5.2 From Institutional Reform to Eschatological Hope

The redemptive outcomes in Chapters 3–7 demonstrate that God uses judgment and deliverance to recalibrate nations toward justice. Chapter 8 will expand this pattern into a vision of the Ancient of Days and the Son of Man, revealing how individual and corporate repentance feeds into the culminating hope of cosmic renewal. Understanding the interplay between present reforms and future consummation reframes all civic engagement as part of an ongoing eschatological trajectory.

7.5.3 Invitation to Anchor in Enduring Kingdom Promises

Before moving into apocalyptic imagery, readers are encouraged to anchor their hearts in the promises of Daniel's visions: that God's kingdom will outlast every empire, and that faithful witnesses will share in His triumph. This anchoring practice involves revisiting prayer rhythms, fellowship disciplines, and prophetic community structures, ensuring that the hope to come ignites present perseverance. As we turn the page, we carry this hope as both shield and compass.

Conclusion

Daniel's night in the lions' den teaches that faithfulness under pressure does more than secure personal vindication—it reshapes entire systems by revealing their moral dependencies. His unshakable commitment to prayer broke the machinery of political manipulation and compelled an imperial proclamation of God's sovereignty. Today's believers, facing subtle and overt restrictions on conscience, draw strength from his example of gentle yet unyielding conviction, strategic legal awareness, and vocational excellence. By embedding visible devotional rhythms, forming tight-knit support circles, and practicing voluntary simplicity, modern disciples prepare themselves for challenges that demand both resilience and grace. In the echo of roaring lions, Daniel's legacy reminds us that steadfast prayer and principled witness can turn even the fiercest opposition into an opportunity for God's power to shine.

Chapter 8 – Vision of the Ages: Apocalyptic Hope and Eschatological Courage

Apocalyptic vision pierces the veil of history's turmoil to reveal a tapestry woven by divine wisdom and cosmic purpose. Daniel's later chapters invite us into a realm where empires appear as beastly reflections of human ambition, and angelic beings contend for the fate of nations. In these symbolic narratives, the Sovereign of eternity presides over chaos, appoints the Son of Man to everlasting reign, and inscribes a precise timetable for redemption. Such revelations were never meant to satisfy mere curiosity about end-times trivia; they are lifelines of courage for believers who face shifting powers and mounting pressures. By decoding these rich symbols—horned beasts, heavenly courtrooms, precise day counts—Daniel calls his readers to stand firm, to intercede with informed hearts, and to align their lives with the unstoppable advance of God's kingdom. This chapter unpacks those visions, mapping their ancient context onto today's struggles, and shows how hope framed by eternity empowers Christians to persevere with joyful confidence.

8.0 Reading Apocalyptic—Why Symbolic Visions Matter for Everyday Saints

8.0.1 Literary DNA of Apocalypse: Heavenly Journey, Symbolic Bestiary, Angelic Interpreters Apocalyptic writing blends story and symbol to pull back the curtain on heaven's perspective, inviting readers to glimpse realities normally hidden behind the fabric of ordinary time. In Daniel 7–12, the prophet is transported—sometimes bodily, sometimes in dream—to cosmic courtrooms, turbulent seas, and star-lit battlefields where history's conflicts appear as prowling beasts and clashing princes. These scenes echo earlier visions given to Ezekiel by the Kebar River and anticipate John's Patmos revelations, forming a literary lineage of unveiling. The bizarre menagerie of lion-bear-leopard hybrids is not meant to confuse but to compress centuries of imperial brutality into single snapshots—visual theology that can be memorized more readily than diplomatic chronicles. Angelic guides such as Gabriel function as tour-hosts, translating bewildering sights into digestible teaching and underscoring that interpretation is a grace, not a human invention. The heavenly journey reminds Israel that earthly geography is not ultimate; a throne higher than Nebuchadnezzar's governs borders and timelines. By using collage-like symbolism rather than plain prose, apocalypse weans the faithful from surface appearances and trains the imagination to expect God's sudden interventions. This genre thus re-enchants the moral imagination, assuring exiles that their struggle is nested inside a vaster drama already scripted for righteousness to prevail.

8.0.2 Discerning Genre Markers to Avoid Sensationalism and Cultivate Watchful Wisdom Because apocalyptic texts rely on hyper-symbolic language, readers must handle them with literary tools suited to their design—much as sailors learn constellations rather than highway signs. Repetition of numbers like seven, ten, and twelve signals completeness or covenant rather than mathematical code to predict news-headlines. Composite monsters borrow imagery from earlier Scripture—Leviathan in Job, Pharaoh's crocodile persona in Ezekiel—so that new visions reverberate with canonical memory. Heavenly courtrooms recall Sinai's thunderous revelation, attributing legal solidity to God's judgments. Recognizing these markers helps believers resist sensationalist timelines that flatten symbolism into newspaper speculation. When visions reference "time, times, and half a time," the phrase marks divinely limited oppression, not a secret calendar hidden in stock charts. Genre sensitivity liberates the church from fear-mongering and equips it for sober perseverance, as Jesus urged His disciples to read "the signs of the times" without chasing date predictions (Matthew 24:36). Proper exegesis yields steady hope instead of anxious calculations, enabling communities to discern real beasts—ideologies that devour the weak—rather than chase prophetic mirages.

8.0.3 Three Lenses: Historical Horizon, Messianic Fulfillment, Ultimate Consummation Apocalyptic vision operates like a prophetic telescope with three nested lenses that sharpen focus at different distances. The historical horizon identifies immediate or near-future events—for Daniel, the rise of Persia, Greece, and Rome—that prove God already steers world affairs (Daniel 8:20-22). The messianic lens telescopes further to the first advent of the Son of Man, when Jesus quotes Daniel to describe His own authority before the Sanhedrin (Mark 14:62). Finally, the ultimate consummation lens stretches to the resurrection of the righteous and final judgment (Daniel 12:2-3), promising cosmic re-creation beyond present epochs. Holding all three lenses together prevents chronological myopia that collapses prophecy into one era and guards against futurism that ignores God's past faithfulness. Past fulfillment authenticates the message, present application energizes discipleship, and future hope inoculates against despair. This layered reading equips believers to live wisely in every generation, confident that God's timetable integrates temporal setbacks into an eternal victory.

8.0.4 Devotional Posture: Humility, Repentance, and Hopeful Imagination Approaching apocalyptic literature demands a heart posture as intentional as scholarly method. Humility bows before mysteries that exceed human calculation, echoing Daniel's confession that "no wisdom resides in me" apart from divine revelation (Daniel 2:30). Repentance surfaces when visions expose communal sins—idolatry, oppression, complacency—and invite the prayerful contrition modeled in Daniel 9. Hopeful imagination rises as the Spirit uses vivid imagery to seed courage, so saints envision reality governed by thrones of fire rather than by claws of beasts. Devotional reading thus becomes resistance training, retraining affections to long for the kingdom that cannot be shaken (Hebrews 12:28). Small-group liturgies—public reading of Daniel 7, silent reflection, communal lament, and responsive praise—translate cosmic scenes into formative worship habits. By blending study with adoration, the church learns to embody the very future it anticipates, turning apocalyptic pages into living rehearsal for the reign of God.

This posture prepares us to step into Daniel's first great vision of the four beasts and the Ancient of Days.

8.1 The Four Beasts and the Ancient of Days (Daniel 7)

8.1.1 Night Visions on the Wind-Tossed Sea Daniel's first apocalyptic dream erupts during Belshazzar's reign, a period of cultural exhaustion when political propaganda insisted Babylon was invincible. In the vision a storm-lashed sea churns beneath moonlight, invoking Genesis chaos imagery and signaling a world out of covenant order (Genesis 1:2). Four grotesque creatures emerge sequentially: a winged lion, a bear with ribs protruding from bloody jaws, a four-winged leopard, and an indescribable iron-toothed monster with ten horns. Each beast compresses an empire's ethos—Babylon's stately grandeur, Persia's devouring conquest, Greece's lightning speed, Rome's iron discipline—without naming them, allowing the symbols to transcend any single regime. These hybrid predators dramatize what happens when political power severs itself from divine stewardship: it devolves into bestial appetite. Ancient readers would have felt visceral dread at such imagery, recognizing how imperial propaganda masked monstrous realities lived daily by subjugated peoples. The rising sequence conveys acceleration: every new empire surpasses the last in efficiency yet also in brutality, teaching that progress without holiness intensifies oppression. This night scene thus sets the stage for heaven's intervention, reminding readers that cosmic storms do not surprise the One who hovers above the flood (Psalm 29:10).

8.1.2 Courtroom Scene with Fiery Thrones Abruptly the camera pans from the turbulent sea to a radiant courtroom where thrones ablaze with wheels of fire are set in place. The Ancient of Days, robed in snow-white garments and hair like pure wool, takes His seat as rivers of flame pour from His presence (Daniel 7:9-10). Books open—divine ledgers itemizing every imperial cruelty and hidden injustice. Millions of angelic attendants stand ready to execute verdicts, underscoring that heaven's bureaucracy dwarfs any earthly administration. This juxtaposition between chaotic sea and ordered court assures persecuted believers that history ends not in anarchy but in adjudication. God's fiery throne evokes Sinai's theophany and Ezekiel's chariot vision, harmonizing legal, prophetic, and priestly motifs. Judgment begins with the slaying of the fourth beast, whose boastful horn—symbol of arrogant authority—is stripped of power. The scene teaches that empires die the moment heaven pronounces sentence, even if earthly fallout takes time to manifest. For disciples under oppressive regimes, this courtroom assures them that dossiers of suffering are not lost; they await a docket where justice will be served without appeal. The fiery throne pre-figures Revelation 20's Great White Throne, connecting Daniel's vision to the New-Testament hope of final judgment.

8.1.3 The Son of Man's Coronation Out of the divine courtroom comes a startling image: one "like a son of man" riding the clouds, a motif reserved in the Old Testament for Yahweh alone (Psalm 104:3). The anthropomorphic radiant figure receives authority, glory, and everlasting dominion directly from the Ancient of Days (Daniel 7:13-14). Early Jewish interpretations linked this figure to messianic expectations; Jesus unapologetically applies the title to Himself before the high priest, merging humanity and divinity in His person. The cloud-borne coronation reverses the beastly ascent from the sea: while monsters rise by clawing, the Son of Man is exalted by divine gift. His kingdom transcends ethnic borders, promising genuine justice rather than imposed peace. For Christians, this coronation validates Christ's resurrection and ascension, the historical pivot after which believers owe ultimate allegiance to no earthly Caesar. The Son of Man's reign also dignifies human vocation: redeemed humanity shares in royal stewardship rather than predatory rule. Daniel's vision thus reorients hope from temporary political reforms to participation in Messiah's unending kingdom.

8.1.4 Saints Possess the Kingdom Angel interpreters clarify that the holy ones of the Most High will receive and possess the kingdom forever (Daniel 7:18). This transfer of dominion from monsters to saints underscores God's original creation mandate—for humanity to govern creation benevolently (Genesis 1:28). The text calls persecuted communities to see themselves not as hunted refugees but as heirs awaiting investiture. The promise shapes ethical stamina: because the kingdom is certain, believers can endure present losses without capitulation. Suffering becomes a birth-pang, not a death-knell (Romans 8:18). Early church fathers read this passage during baptisms, reminding catechumens that joining Christ means inheriting a throne of service. Modern disciples glean courage for civic engagement, resisting tyranny by anticipating a future where meekness, not aggression, administers the world. The angel's assurance links to Revelation 5:10, where redeemed people reign on earth, forming a canonical symphony of eschatological vocation. Thus the vision does not fuel escapism but galvanizes holy activism, confident that their labor in the Lord is not in vain (1 Corinthians 15:58).

8.2 Ram, Goat, and the Little Horn (Daniel 8)

8.2.1 Geographic Focus—From Babylon to Susa Two years after the chapter 7 dream, Daniel finds himself "in the citadel of Susa," capital of Persia (Daniel 8:2). The vision's new location signals a geographic handoff from Babylonian supremacy to Persian ascendancy, anchoring symbols in real geopolitical transitions. Standing by the Ulai Canal, Daniel watches as history rewrites its map; canals once used for commerce become prophetic stages. The shift of scenery reminds readers that God's concern spans entire regions, not just Judah's little patch of land. Susa later becomes the backdrop of Esther's story and Nehemiah's cupbearing, tying disparate biblical narratives into a single providential thread. By embedding Daniel's vision in a recognizable Persian setting, Scripture affirms that apocalyptic hope speaks to concrete political realities rather than abstract spiritualism. This local color primes Daniel—and us—for a zoom-lens prophecy that examines the next centuries in surgical detail.

8.2.2 Clash of Horned Powers Daniel sees a ram with two horns—one higher than the other—charging west, north, and south without opposition. Gabriel later explains that the ram signifies the Medo-Persian coalition, the taller horn representing Persia's eventual dominance (Daniel 8:20). Suddenly a male goat with a prominent single horn races from the west, shattering the ram. This goat is Greece, and its horn symbolizes Alexander the Great's meteoric rise (Daniel 8:21). The vivid animal duel compresses decades of military campaigns into seconds of symbolic combat, illustrating how swiftly empires shift. The goat's unstoppable speed depicts Alexander's rapid conquests across Asia Minor, Egypt, and Persia. Yet the prominent horn breaks prematurely—Alexander's untimely death at thirty-three—followed by four horns growing in its place, mapping onto the Diadochi's division of his empire. This portrayal teaches that power gathered through human genius still submits to divine limits, echoing Isaiah 40:23's claim that God reduces princes to nothing. Observing these horned clashes encourages believers to interpret headlines through providence's lens, recognizing that no political juggernaut outpaces God's sovereignty.

8.2.3 Rise of the Insolent King Out of one of the successor horns emerges a "little horn" that grows exceedingly great toward the Beautiful Land, desecrating sanctuary worship (Daniel 8:9-12). History identifies this insolent king as Antiochus IV Epiphanes, who outlawed Torah, erected an altar to Zeus in the temple, and slaughtered a pig on it—actions triggering the Maccabean revolt. Daniel's vision labels him a "master of intrigue" who prospers by cunning rather than sheer force (Daniel 8:25), highlighting a shift from overt military conquest to manipulative cultural oppression. Antiochus embodies a prototype of antichrist figures: leaders who exalt themselves above all gods, attack covenant identity, and weaponize policy to smother worship. His reign, though intense, is limited by God's decree—"but he will be broken, and that without human hand" (Daniel 8:25). The pattern offers pastoral insight: persecution may peak under charismatic tyrants, yet divine sovereignty caps their tenure. This prepares believers to recognize recurring "little horns" in different eras—totalitarian ideologues, technocratic utopians, or consumerist leviathans—and to endure by recalling the impermanence of oppressive regimes.

8.2.4 Sanctuaries, Timetables, and Ultimate Cleansing Daniel hears holy ones debate, "How long?" before truth prevails, and receives the cryptic answer: "2,300 evenings and mornings; then the sanctuary shall be restored" (Daniel 8:13-14). Scholars debate whether this period equals 1,150 daily sacrifices or 2,300 full days, but all agree it predicts a finite span culminating in Hanukkah's rededication of the temple (164 BC). This timetable reassures the faithful that desecration carries an expiration date; God tracks injustice to the very sunrise and sunset. The cleansing foreshadows Christ's ultimate temple cleansing during Passion Week and His promise to rebuild a sanctuary not made with hands (John 2:19-21). Apocalyptic chronology, therefore, is less about secret codes and more about moral clocks heralding holy restoration. Gabriel's mandate to "seal up the vision" signals that fulfillment will vindicate prophecy across centuries, inviting each generation to watch for echoes of Antiochus in new guises. The sanctuary's eventual purification mirrors the closing scene of Revelation, where no temple is needed because God and the Lamb illuminate the city (Revelation 21:22-23). Thus Daniel 8 integrates detailed historical prediction with eschatological anticipation, affirming that every profaned altar and broken heart awaits comprehensive cleansing in the age to come.

8.3 Seventy Weeks Prophecy (Daniel 9)

8.3.1 Daniel's Scripture-Fed Lament and Intercession Daniel's vision of calibrated redemption begins not in an angelic flash but in the quiet labor of Bible study. Having survived two empires, the prophet reads Jeremiah's letter to the exiles and discovers that the promised seventy-year exile is drawing to a close (Jeremiah 29:10–14). The text ignites a cascade of prayerful grief; instead of triumphal celebration, Daniel turns to sackcloth, ashes, and fasting. His posture teaches that prophecy is not a spectator sport—it summons the faithful to repentant dialogue with God. He confesses corporate sin with first-person plurality—"we have sinned, we have rebelled"—refusing to distance himself from national guilt (Daniel 9:5). By rehearsing covenant history—from Exodus mercy to exile discipline—he anchors plea in God's proven character. Daniel's lament blends petition and praise, weaving together phrases from Deuteronomy, Psalms, and Chronicles, showing that biblical language becomes the grammar of effective intercession. Such Scripture-fed prayer counters the modern tendency to approach God with raw emotion unshaped by revelation. It also demonstrates that accurate eschatology feeds profound humility: seeing the timetable does not breed entitlement but deep contrition. Daniel's example urges contemporary disciples to let biblical promises drive confession rather than presumption, forming hearts ready to receive angelic insight.

8.3.2 Gabriel's Four-Segment Timeline In response to that prayer, the archangel Gabriel arrives "in swift flight" at the time of the evening offering, signaling divine attentiveness to liturgical hours (Daniel 9:21). Gabriel outlines a seventy-sevens timetable subdivided into three phases: seven sevens, sixty-two sevens, and a final seven. The first segment begins with a decree to rebuild Jerusalem, probably the edict of Artaxerxes to Ezra (Ezra 7:11–26). The second covers an extended era of ordinary history in which city and temple exist amid "troubled times," reflecting Persia's tolerance and later Hellenistic pressures. The final seven is unique, packed with messianic drama and covenant conflict. By structuring time this way, Gabriel reframes years as sabbatical units, tethering eschatology to rhythms of rest and release. The angel's precision dissolves superstition: God partitions history with clock-maker care, reassuring exiles that chaos is neither random nor supreme. Moreover, the segmented scheme answers Daniel's plea for mercy by promising that divine action will exceed the mere end of exile; it will culminate in atonement that abolishes transgression (Daniel 9:24). Gabriel's timeline thus converts lament into structured hope, modeling how revelation clarifies rather than confuses when received in prayer-soaked humility.

8.3.3 Messiah, Covenant, and Catastrophe Gabriel's message centers on one astonishing statement: after sixty-two sevens, "the Anointed One will be cut off and will have nothing" (Daniel 9:26). This verse anticipates Christ's crucifixion—Messiah executed seemingly abandoned, yet accomplishing redemption. The prophecy then foretells a coming ruler who destroys city and sanctuary, an allusion to Rome's AD 70 siege that leveled Herod's temple. Thus, the final week juxtaposes covenant faithfulness in the suffering Servant with covenant desecration by imperial legions. Halfway through that week, sacrifice ceases, pointing to both Calvary's once-for-all offering and the temple's later ruin. Catastrophe, therefore, is not the last word; it becomes the stage where atonement eclipses ritual shadows. Daniel's vision pits two covenants against each other: one secured by Messiah's blood, the other shattered by idolatrous power. The narrative warns that those who reject the Anointed One align themselves with forces that desolate worship rather than renew it. Yet the same timeline promises that righteousness will ultimately fill the age, confirming Paul's claim that "all God's promises are 'Yes' in Christ" (2 Corinthians 1:20). Understanding this interplay prepares believers to face tribulation with eyes fixed on a crucified yet reigning King.

8.3.4 Measuring Jubilee Hope Seventy sevens equal four-hundred-ninety years—ten jubilee cycles—signaling a super-jubilee when debts are forgiven on a cosmic scale (Leviticus 25). Gabriel's arithmetic transforms an agricultural festival into a metronome of eschatological hope. The climax involves six divine actions: finishing transgression, ending sin, atoning iniquity, bringing everlasting righteousness, sealing vision, and anointing the holy place (Daniel 9:24). Each verb completes what jubilee foreshadowed: release from bondage, restitution of inheritance, rest in God's presence. Daniel's generation saw only the embryonic fulfillment in temple rebuilding, but the gospel community recognizes Jesus proclaiming "good news to the poor" as jubilee incarnate (Luke 4:18-19). The prophecy invites saints to live jubilee ethics now—canceling debts, rescuing trafficked workers, forgiving personal wrongs—as rehearsal for the kingdom's full arrival. Thus, meticulous timetables nurture embodied compassion rather than escapist chronologizing. This jubilee horizon transitions us naturally into Daniel's final trilogy of visions, where cosmic warfare and resurrection stretch hope beyond history's horizon.

8.4 Final Conflict and Resurrection (Daniel 10–12)

8.4.1 Angelic Warfare Behind Political Headlines Daniel fasts for twenty-one days by the Tigris when a radiant being—likely Gabriel or a Christophany—reveals that Persian and Greek "princes" have delayed angelic missions (Daniel 10:12-13). The text unveils a meta-political realm where supernatural entities influence empires, turning diplomatic negotiations into spiritual battlegrounds. Michael, Israel's guardian, contends with these regional powers, ensuring that covenant promises outlast earthly intrigues. The scene teaches that believers' prayers affect this unseen theater, encouraging intercession as strategic partnership rather than pious ritual. Understanding angelic warfare reframes discouraging news cycles as invitations to spiritual vigilance; geopolitical tremors echo clashes in heavenly councils. The episode dismantles secular materialism by asserting that policy shifts are not solely human calculations but responses to invisible hierarchies. Daniel's trembling and strengthening by angelic touch illustrate how divine empowerment equips frail mortals to receive weighty revelations. His experience calls modern disciples to both realism and prayerful boldness, knowing that God's emissaries battle beyond our perception yet respond to our petitions.

8.4.2 Time, Times, and Half a Time The vision introduces enigmatic periods: a "time, times, and half a time," 1,290 days, and 1,335 days (Daniel 12:7, 11-12). These symbolic intervals mark seasons of intensified persecution truncated by divine decree. Scholars note that three-and-a-half years equals half of seven, signifying incomplete oppression. The additional 45 days between 1,290 and 1,335 invite perseverance beyond expected relief, rewarding those who trust during delay. Such elasticity inoculates against rigid date-setting while affirming that suffering is measured, not infinite. Theologically, the intervals echo Elijah's drought (1 Kings 17-18) and Christ's ministry of three-and-a-half years, presenting tribulation as precursor to prophetic vindication. For modern believers, these numbers function as spiritual chronotherapy, teaching that endurance often requires staying faithful a little longer than anticipated. Practical discipleship may involve building spiritual margins—Sabbath rhythms, emergency prayer partners—to outlast institutional pressure. When deliverance seems overdue, Daniel's calibrated chronology whispers, "Blessed is the one who waits" (Daniel 12:12).

8.4.3 Shattering of the Holy People Daniel hears that final events culminate when "the power of the holy people has been finally broken" (Daniel 12:7). This somber line counters triumphalist readings of faith by predicting a period when God allows His community to reach the end of human resourcefulness. Shattering, however, serves redemptive refinement, separating alloy from gold as in Zechariah's furnace prophecy (Zechariah 13:9). Persecution exposes false security, compelling saints to rely wholly on resurrection hope. Church history confirms this pattern: Roman arenas, Soviet gulags, and contemporary martyrdoms purify witness while expanding gospel influence. The shattering motif cautions against equating cultural dominance with kingdom success, reminding believers that weakness can be the crucible of glory (2 Corinthians 12:9). Recognizing this dynamic prepares communities to embrace vulnerability as a strategic posture in spiritual warfare, setting the stage for the resurrection promise that crowns the vision.

8.4.4 Awakening from the Dust Daniel receives what is arguably the Old Testament's clearest statement of bodily resurrection: "Multitudes who sleep in the dust of the earth will awake" (Daniel 12:2). Some rise to everlasting life, others to shame—introducing moral bifurcation that assures ultimate justice. The imagery reverses Genesis 3's curse—returning to dust—by declaring dust a temporary dormitory, not a final sentence. The righteous shine like stars, echoing Abraham's promise and Paul's celestial resurrection glory (Philippians 3:21). Resurrection hope propels ethical urgency; knowing deeds echo into eternity, wise teachers "turn many to righteousness" (Daniel 12:3). This promise liberates the oppressed from fear of annihilation: even if beasts devour the body or regimes erase names, God will reconstitute identity with honor. Early rabbis and church fathers drew courage from this verse, framing martyrdom as sowing seeds that burst into immortal bloom. Contemporary disciples, confronting nihilistic narratives, can anchor mental health and social activism in the certainty that no sacrifice for justice is lost to history's abyss. Daniel's closing exhortation to "go your way till the end" (Daniel 12:13) affirms vocation until rest, linking resurrection doctrine with daily faithfulness.

8.5 How Apocalyptic Vision Shapes Present Conduct

8.5.1 Hope as Moral Catalyst Apocalyptic hope is not escapist optimism but kinetic energy that launches believers into sacrificial love. Knowing the kingdom is secure frees disciples to risk reputation, comfort, and even life for the marginalized. John reminds the church that seeing the coming glory motivates purity now (1 John 3:2-3). Similarly, Daniel's expectancy fueled decades of incorruptible service in pagan courts. Hope reconfigures moral cost-benefit analyses: generosity, chastity, and truth-telling outweigh short-term gain because eternity recalibrates value systems. Youth ministries that teach eschatology alongside social justice produce servants who resist burnout, viewing setbacks as temporary turbulence on a guaranteed flight path. In counseling, resurrection hope breaks the cycle of despair, offering meaning to suffering that secular therapy cannot supply. Thus, far from paralyzing believers, apocalyptic vision ignites holy activism.

8.5.2 Living on an Eternal Timeline To live eschatologically means placing daily choices on a continuum that stretches beyond death. Budget sheets become mission statements when money is seen as seed for an everlasting harvest (Matthew 6:19-21). Career planning shifts from ladder-climbing to kingdom leverage, asking how skills serve the Son of Man's reign. Time management favors disciplines—prayer, study, hospitality—that build eternal dividends. Even recreation is reframed as Sabbath anticipation rather than escapist binge. Families set rhythms of intercessory prayer for unreached peoples, treating global evangelization as a pending inheritance. Churches budget for creation care, anticipating a renewed earth, thereby embodying their future home's values. Living on an eternal timeline preserves joy in adversity: chronic illness becomes a chapter, not the entire book; persecution, a paragraph in an epic. This temporal elasticity produces resilience and patience, countering the culture's tyranny of the urgent.

8.5.3 Discernment over Despair Apocalyptic literature often births two opposite errors: fear-mongering and apathetic detachment. Daniel's balanced approach—lamenting evil yet proclaiming divine sovereignty—models discernment that resists both extremes. Discernment asks which contemporary ideologies bear beast-like traits—dehumanization, idolatry of technology, or economic exploitation—and calls them out without hysteria. It also distinguishes genuine prophetic warnings from clickbait alarmism, applying criteria like Christocentric hope and biblical coherence. Community think-tanks, comprised of theologians, economists, and artists, can produce discernment briefs guiding congregations through ethical quagmires. Spiritual disciplines of silence and examen tune hearts to the Spirit's gentle correctives rather than media-induced panic. Discernment filters consumption habits: believers evaluate news sources, social feeds, and entertainment through the lens of Daniel's visions, retaining that which edifies and discarding seductive despair. Thus, apocalyptic wisdom equips saints to navigate complexity with calm courage.

8.5.4 Communities of Interpretive Wisdom Daniel never processed visions alone; heavenly interpreters and earthly companions created a hermeneutical community. Today, house churches, seminaries, and intergenerational forums can function as "Daniel collectives," pooling gifts of prophecy, scholarship, and mercy. Such communities study texts contextually, cross-checking interpretations to avoid private speculation. They practice liturgies that rehearse the cosmic story—Advent longing, Easter triumph, Pentecost empowerment—embedding theology in communal memory. Story-sharing nights allow members to relate personal experiences of God's deliverance to scriptural paradigms, reinforcing interpretive confidence. Communities also cultivate young "apocalyptic literates," teaching symbolic reading through art projects and digital storytelling. When crises hit—a pandemic, political unrest—these networks release timely statements rooted in hope, guiding public witness. They foster global connections, learning from persecuted believers whose lived experience of beastly regimes sharpens Western understanding. By embodying interpretive wisdom collectively, the church fulfills Daniel's call that "those who are wise will instruct many" (Daniel 11:33), turning apocalyptic insight into tangible guidance for a fragmented world.

8.6 Pilgrims of Hope in a Fragmented World

8.6.1 Daniel's Survival Paves the Way for Cosmic Visions

Daniel's dramatic rescue from the lions' den not only vindicates his private devotion but also qualifies him to bear the weight of unprecedented prophetic insight. Having proven faithful under threat of death, he can credibly convey visions that span centuries and transcend human comprehension. His deliverance functions as a living parable: when earth's dens and campaigns seem victorious, God's faithful remnant still stands unscathed by his sovereign protection (Psalm 91:13). This precedent teaches that perseverance under systemic opposition precedes revelatory commissioning. The angelic messenger who stirred lions to sleep now announces visions of beasts, horns, and resurrection, underscoring that cosmic disclosure reserves first place for those tested by tribulation. For modern readers, Daniel's trajectory suggests that the crucible of personal trials refines the capacity to receive and interpret apocalyptic revelation. The trajectory from court advisor to apocalyptic seer also models a vocational arc where faithfulness in small things leads to stewardship of greater mysteries (Luke 16:10). Communities that cultivate endurance through prayer and solidarity thus prepare themselves for the unfolding of God's redemptive plan. Just as Daniel's unshaken character enabled him to grasp the meaning of four beasts and seventy weeks, today's disciples can condition their hearts to embrace eschatological hope by passing through their own "den" experiences. This bridge invites reflection on how individual and corporate trials become the fertile ground for cultivating prophetic imagination and charting pilgrim pathways toward the new creation.

8.6.2 From Institutional Reform to Eschatological Hope

The victories Daniel won in palace protocols—dietary bans overturned, prayer decrees rescinded, imperial protections declared—exemplify how God can reform human systems to honor righteousness. Yet his subsequent apocalyptic visions remind us that institutional renewal remains provisional pending ultimate consummation. Temporal reforms clear space for justice and mercy, foreshadowing the final establishment of the kingdom of God. When Daniel sees the Ancient of Days enthroned and the beasts destroyed, he discerns that every policy shift and legal adjustment anticipates a cosmic realignment of all creation. This spectrum from civic correction to eternal restoration invites believers to marry activism with ascetic anticipation. Reform without hope of consummation risks mere humanism; hope without attention to structural sin lapses into escapism. By integrating these elements, Daniel's life exemplifies balanced discipleship: engage in policy change as a foretaste, while intensifying prayerful preparation for the day when "time shall be no more" (Revelation 10:6). Communities animated by this dual vision invest in short-term advocacy—anti-corruption initiatives, economic justice campaigns—while sustaining long-term formation: sabbaths, reports of answered prayer, and liturgies that reorient heart toward the age to come. This dynamic continuity between reform and hope equips pilgrims to walk steadfastly in a world where empires rise and fall but God's kingdom advances unimpeded.

8.6.3 Invitation to Anchor in Enduring Kingdom Promises

Before launching into practical pathways for twenty-first-century pilgrims, readers are invited to anchor themselves in the bedrock promises unveiled in Daniel's visions. These anchors include the certainty of resurrection beyond the grave, the assurance of judgment executed by the Ancient of Days, and the inheritance shared by saints who persevere. Journaling exercises help individuals chart personal commitments alongside these promises: declaring which covenant truths they will memorize, which patterns of prayer they will sustain, and which justice initiatives they will support until Christ's return. Small groups might craft a communal "Eschatological Rule of Life," specifying weekly rhythms, quarterly retreats, and annual fasts that embody Daniel's devotional trajectory. This rule situates personal goals within the church's calendrical cycle—Advent longing, Lenten repentance, Pentecostal empowerment—ensuring that apocalyptic hope continually reenergizes daily disciplines. Participants also identify potential "lions' dens" in their vocations and plan spiritual contingencies: prayer circles, legal advisors, mentorship networks. Digital platforms can host shared calendars for prayer windows and Scripture sprints, forging virtual pilgrim bands across continents. Such anchoring practices transform abstract eschatological doctrines into embodied commitments, enabling believers to live as pilgrims whose final city lies beyond the stars. By anchoring in kingdom promises, faith communities become resilient waystations of hope for a fragmented world, ready to move into the final chapter of practical discipleship.

Conclusion

Daniel's apocalyptic panoramas remind us that the trials of our era—political upheaval, cultural decay, personal suffering—are but the prelude to a grand consummation in which justice flows like rivers and mourning is no more. The beasts we fear, the horns that threaten, and the shadows that loom all submit to the Ancient of Days, whose sovereign Word renders every tyrant's roar into silence. As we walk forward, equipped with symbolic lenses and anchored in resurrection hope, we discover that true courage is not the absence of fear but the certainty of victory secured by the One who conquers both death and time. Embracing this vision, believers become pilgrims of hope, living today in the light of tomorrow's glory and advancing a kingdom that will never be shaken.

Chapter 9 – Walking Against the World Today: Contemporary Issues and Biblical Wisdom

In an era defined by digital distractions, moral ambiguity, and relentless pressure to conform, the call to walk against prevailing currents has never been more urgent. Like exiles in a foreign land, today's believers navigate a landscape where truth is contested, bodies are commodified, data defines identity, money wields hidden sway, and political loyalties fracture communities. Yet Daniel's journey through palace intrigue, fiery trials, and prophetic visions offers a timeless blueprint: cultivate private rhythms that sustain public witness, anchor convictions in covenant truth, and translate ancient disciplines into creative resistance. This chapter engages the pressing challenges of our age—secular skepticism, redefined gender norms, surveillance economies, economic anxieties, and polarized politics—and explores how biblical wisdom equips Christians to stand firm with both compassion and clarity. By integrating prayer, study, ethical formation, and communal solidarity, disciples become agents of renewal, embodying the kingdom's subversive hope amid a world clamoring for conformity.

9.0 Exiles in Every Epoch—Why Daniel's Model Still Speaks

Every generation of believers discovers that exile is not merely a geographical dislocation but a spiritual condition in which prevailing values strain, mute, or mock covenant loyalty. From first-century churches navigating Caesar worship to twenty-first-century disciples negotiating secular humanism, the atmosphere of cultural pressure remains strikingly familiar. Daniel's memoirs sketch an enduring template: carve out rhythms of prayer, cultivate intellectual excellence, and embody prophetic critique even while serving pagan institutions. His habits demonstrate that holiness is portable; it survives palace intrigue, ideological propaganda, and shifting administrations because it is rooted in communion rather than circumstance. Modern Christians face comparable "statues" when social media algorithms enshrine self-promotion as ultimate good, when "furnaces" of cancel culture threaten professional ruin for dissent, and when "lions' dens" of regulatory boards examine conscience for signs of nonconformity. Diagnosing these arenas requires a grid that assesses three dimensions of any cultural demand: Does it distort truth, degrade image-bearers, or dethrone God? If the answer is yes, Daniel's strategy activates—conviction that resists, compassion that intercedes, and creative resistance that seeks the city's welfare even while challenging its idols. His legacy debunks the myth that faithfulness must equal withdrawal; instead, it models redemptive participation shaped by unbreakable allegiance to the Ancient of Days. By threading courageous witness through exemplary competence, Daniel earned a voice in policy without surrendering prophetic edge, showing that excellence and dissent can coexist. That combination still disarms critics today, because institutions rarely know how to silence employees whose work outshines rivals even as their conscience outlasts decrees. The chapter ahead unfolds how these core disciplines apply to contested fields—philosophy classrooms, sexual ethics debates, surveillance economies, financial markets, and partisan arenas—offering practical pathways for saints determined to walk against the world without abandoning it.

9.1 Secularism and Moral Relativism

9.1.1 Marketplace of Competing Truth Claims The digital age has transformed every smartphone into a souk of competing worldviews, where TikTok life-coaches preach self-curated spirituality one swipe away from nihilist comedians who deconstruct meaning for laughs. Newsfeeds algorithmically personalize reality, delivering echo-chamber facts that confirm existing intuitions and brand doubt as moral virtue. University freshmen encounter syllabi proclaiming that grand narratives died with modernity, only to discover that micro-narratives now wield near-total authority over identity formation. In this cacophony, truth is measured not by correspondence to reality but by the number of retweets, likes, or citations from celebrity pundits. Secularism thrives in ambiguity, proposing that public reason must bracket metaphysical claims, yet smuggling in its own creed of expressive individualism. Daniel's Babylon likewise sponsored a pluralistic meta-festival of gods, each claiming sphere sovereignty while the empire insisted none may assert exclusive supremacy. Recognizing parallels, believers today must learn to decode cultural liturgies that teach students to confess, "My truth," instead of, "The Lord is God" (Deuteronomy 6:4). The marketplace metaphor also reveals economic drivers: attention is monetized, so controversy outsells contemplation, pushing nuanced conviction to the margins. Unchecked, this climate nurtures cynicism, as every moral stance is suspected of hidden power plays, echoing Pilate's weary question, "What is truth?" (John 18:38). Yet pluralism need not fray faith; it can sharpen apologetic skill, compelling Christians to articulate hope with clarity rather than cliché. Marketplace conditions call for discernment that distinguishes legitimate doubt seeking understanding from performative skepticism that markets uncertainty. By naming the idols of novelty and notoriety, the church can reclaim its heritage of reasoned persuasion rooted in the God who cannot lie (Titus 1:2).

9.1.2 Intellectual Fidelity to Scripture If truth is auctioned to the highest influencer, Scripture invites disciples to anchor epistemology in revelation, not virality. Intellectual fidelity means submitting imagination, scholarship, and daily decision-making to the Word that judges every philosophical trend (Hebrews 4:12). This submission is not anti-intellectual; Daniel mastered Chaldean literature without diluting Torah conviction, modeling an integrative posture that reads competing texts through a covenant lens. Contemporary equivalents include theologians engaging evolutionary biology, economists auditing neoliberal assumptions, and artists critiquing postmodern aesthetics—all while confessing the risen Christ as Logos. Fidelity requires tools: historical-grammatical exegesis to avoid proof-texting, canonical synthesis to honor Scripture's grand narrative, and communal interpretation to resist echo-chamber eisegesis. It also demands formation of intellectual virtues—humility to admit gaps, courage to challenge consensus, and charity to represent opponents fairly. Seminary coursework and lay catechesis alike must therefore move beyond doctrinal memorization into habits of critical reading that detect hidden anthropologies beneath policy proposals or advertising scripts. Intellectual fidelity further expresses itself in moral coherence: research ethics, citation honesty, and refusal to plagiarize because truthfulness is worship. When Christian scholars publish peer-reviewed articles that marry rigor with reverence, they incarnate Daniel's testimony that God's wisdom outclasses Babylon's think-tanks tenfold (Daniel 1:20).

9.1.3 Dialoguing without Retreating Secular pluralism tempts believers toward two equal and opposite errors: combative rhetoric that caricatures opponents or self-segregation behind doctrinal walls. Daniel charted a third way by engaging Babylonian sages respectfully, even asking for time to interpret the king's dream on their behalf (Daniel 2:16-18). Dialoguing without retreating begins with relational curiosity—listening to understand worldviews before critiquing inconsistencies. It pursues common-grace bridges, affirming shared longings for justice, beauty, and transcendence as echoes of the imago Dei. This posture grants dignity to conversation partners while maintaining allegiance to revealed truth. Practically, it requires rhetorical discipline: avoiding straw-man fallacies, acknowledging when secular critics expose church hypocrisy, and framing rebuttals around the Gospel's positive vision rather than merely negating rival claims. Forums such as interfaith panels, ethics committees, and social-media threads become laboratories for this practice, each question an invitation to bear witness with "gentleness and respect" (1 Peter 3:15). Dialogical resilience protects against fatigue born of constant ideological sparring by rooting identity in God's unchanging affirmation rather than debate outcomes.

9.1.4 Disciplines of the Informed Mind To navigate a pluralistic landscape, Christians cultivate mental habits that parallel Daniel's disciplined prayer windows. Lectio academicus pairs daily Scripture reading with analysis of one challenging secular text, teaching believers to compare narratives rather than absorb them uncritically. Worldview comparison charts help small groups map how different philosophies answer questions of origin, meaning, morality, and destiny, revealing Christianity's coherence. Hospitable reading groups invite non-Christian friends to discuss classic literature, modeling civil disagreement and reciprocal learning. These practices inoculate against intellectual laziness by normalizing complexity and dialogue. Annual "media sabbaths"—week-long fasts from newsfeeds—reset attention spans eroded by algorithmic scrolling, enabling deep study. Memorizing creeds and catechisms supplies mental furniture that withstands cultural redecorations, much like Daniel's memorized psalms sustained him in Babylon. Conferences on faith and science, art and theology, or economics and ethics expand disciples' intellectual perimeter, proving that all truth is God's truth. Together these disciplines cultivate saints whose minds are renewed, able to test and approve God's will amid shifting cultural scripts (Romans 12:2). The transition from contested truth claims leads naturally into debates over embodiment and sexuality, where convictions move from head to heart and body.

9.2 Sexual Ethics and Gender Ideology

9.2.1 Counter-Cultural Chastity and Human Dignity Western culture's sexual narrative argues that autonomy equals authenticity, reducing the body to a canvas for self-expressive desire. Scripture counters with a robust anthropology: bodies are temples of the Holy Spirit, purchased at a price, destined for resurrection glory (1 Corinthians 6:19-20). Chastity, therefore, is not repression but recalibration of desire toward covenant fidelity and mutual self-gift. In a porn-saturated milieu, abstaining from lust becomes an act of prophetic protest against industries that monetize exploitation. Daniel's dietary refusal in chapter 1 provides a template: he declined Babylon's delicacies to preserve covenant identity, just as disciples today decline voyeuristic appetites to honor the marriage banquet of the Lamb. Counter-cultural chastity also affirms human dignity beyond utility; persons are not consumable experiences but mysteries to be reverenced. This ethic elevates singleness as a vocational gift, not a relational deficit, mirroring Christ's own celibate life. Churches teaching this vision must pair doctrinal clarity with pastoral empathy, acknowledging wounds from sexual brokenness and offering healing liturgies rooted in confession and sacramental grace.

9.2.2 Compassion without Compromise Engaging gender dysphoria and divergent sexual identities demands a tone steeped in Christ's tears over Jerusalem and His call to repent because the kingdom is near (Luke 19:41; Matthew 4:17). Compassion begins with active listening—hearing stories before prescribing answers—recognizing that identity questions often mask layers of rejection and trauma. At the same time, compromise is avoided by anchoring anthropology in creation's binary design and redemption's eschatological marriage of Christ and church (Genesis 1:27; Ephesians 5:31-32). Churches establish care teams trained in trauma-informed ministry, ensuring pastoral conversations hold space for lament as well as exhortation. Policies clarify bathroom access, pronoun usage, and membership expectations with transparent kindness, preventing ad-hoc decisions driven by fear. Disciples study Jesus' encounter with the Samaritan woman, noting His gracious revelation of her history alongside a firm call to transformation (John 4). Compassion without compromise refuses both extremes: affirming culture's fluidity narratives or weaponizing truth in graceless confrontation. It instead offers a third path—inviting all people into a costly yet liberating discipleship under Christ's lordship.

9.2.3 Embodied Liturgies of Purity and Honor Understanding sexuality as worship requires more than new ideas; it requires new rhythms that train the body's reflexes. Fasting from porn algorithms involves installing accountability software, setting communal phone curfews, and publicly celebrating streaks of digital sobriety. Covenant groups of three or four meet weekly for confession of eye-gate temptations, echoing Daniel's peer solidarity with Hananiah, Mishael, and Azariah. Young adults practice "redemptive dating" by integrating community oversight—scheduling group outings before exclusive encounters—to ensure relationships flourish under communal blessing. Married couples employ Sabbath intimacy rituals that celebrate union as a signpost of divine love, reinforcing that eros submits to agape. Church retreats teach theology of the body through dance, art, and guided silence, embedding reverence in muscle memory. These physical liturgies counter cultural scripts that idolize spontaneity by elevating intentionality shaped by covenant vows. Over months, embodied practices reorder affections, enabling believers to present their bodies as living sacrifices, holy and pleasing to God (Romans 12:1).

9.2.4 Public Witness in Policy Arenas Sexual ethics debates extend beyond personal discipleship into legislative battles over marriage definition, parental rights, and medical conscience. Christians trained in Daniel's diplomatic boldness draft amicus briefs, testify before committees, and propose religious-liberty clauses that protect all faiths. Medical professionals facing pressure to perform gender-transition procedures form conscience networks, offering alternative referrals while advocating for patient dignity. Adoption agencies collaborate with secular counterparts to prove that faith-based convictions enhance, not hinder, placement outcomes. In media engagements, believers shift conversations from culture-war sloganeering to gospel hospitality, emphasizing Jesus' invitation to abundant life. When laws conflict with conscience, civil disobedience follows Daniel's pattern—respectful refusal, clear testimony, and acceptance of consequences while trusting God with results. Public witness unites compassion and clarity, showing society that moral conviction can coexist with neighbor-love, and setting the stage for the next discussions on technology's pervasive reach into human identity.

9.3 Technology, Surveillance, and Conformity

9.3.1 Digital Babylon: Algorithms That Shape Desire Smartphone screens glow like miniature ziggurats, summoning users to ritual swipes that form habits faster than most people notice. Each tap deposits data fragments into corporate storehouses where sophisticated algorithms translate attention into profit-yielding predictions. What appears as neutral convenience is in fact an engineered liturgy: push notifications function as digital trumpets, calling the multitude to bow before a flood of curated content. Machine-learning models track dopamine spikes, learning which memes keep you scrolling just a second longer, which political outrage triggers sharing, which purchase patterns signal late-night vulnerability. The result is a discipleship of the subconscious in which affections are quietly re-wired toward self-curation and perpetual consumption. Scripture warns that desire untethered from covenant anchors becomes idolatry, echoing Jeremiah's description of people who "went after worthlessness, and became worthless" (Jeremiah 2:5). The Babylonian court renamed exiles to reshape identity; algorithmic renaming occurs through targeted ads and recommended playlists that tell you who you should become. Gen-Z believers confess difficulty concentrating on prayer because the mind instinctively expects stimulus every eight seconds—precisely the metric most social platforms target. Awareness campaigns in churches illustrate data trails on projected screens, helping congregants visualize how clicks sculpt personal liturgies. Youth groups conduct media diaries for a week, discovering that most members touch their phones more times per day than they pray in a month. Far from demonizing technology, Daniel-shaped wisdom discerns that the issue lies not in the devices but in unexamined surrender of attention. Recognizing digital Babylon's catechesis motivates believers to adopt counter-formation habits rather than drifting into algorithmic conformity.

9.3.2 Practising Sabbath and Data Silence Sabbath in a surveillance economy becomes an act of cultural rebellion, declaring that human worth exceeds productivity metrics and engagement statistics. Families power down Wi-Fi routers from sundown Friday to sundown Saturday, rediscovering board games and unhurried meals as liturgies of presence. Monastic-inspired offices create device lockers at the entry, signaling that employees may think deeply without checking Slack every five minutes. Church retreat centers host "48-hour disconnects," collecting participants' phones in sealed bags while providing analog Bibles and blank journals, cultivating an attentiveness many attendees have not felt since childhood. Data silence also includes strategic un-subscriptions: believers audit mailing lists and social feeds, trimming voices that inflame outrage while following Philippians 4:8's guideline for thoughts that are true, noble, and lovely. Digital sabbaths incorporate small-scale craftsmanship—garden work, bread baking, calligraphy—that reacquaint body and soul with tactile creation. Some households hang cloth over television screens during Advent and Lent, reminding inhabitants that spiritual seasons outrank entertainment cycles. Testimonies report lower anxiety and better sleep after even incremental practice of weekly tech-free windows. As Israelites learned wilderness dependence by gathering manna only six days, modern disciples learn trust by letting email accumulate for a day, believing God sustains reputations and opportunities without perpetual self-promotion. Data silence becomes not absence but space in which the still small voice pierces through pings and vibrations, much like Elijah hearing God's whisper after the earthquake and fire (1 Kings 19:12).

9.3.3 Designing for Dignity A growing cohort of Christian engineers and UX designers view their work as an extension of Imago Dei ethics, refusing to build features that exploit vulnerabilities. They convene online guilds that share open-source code for privacy-forward analytics, proving that corporations can thrive without surveillance capitalism. In university hackathons, student teams prototype social networks that limit daily scroll time, award points for logging off, and default to chronological feeds rather than outrage-amplifying algorithms. Hospitals deploy patient portals coded to minimize data harvesting, integrating medical confidentiality with Proverbs 11:13's principle of trustworthy secrecy. Faith-led investors use shareholder resolutions to pressure tech giants toward transparent algorithm disclosures, arguing from Psalm 139:1-4 that divine omniscience liberates humans, whereas corporate pseudo-omniscience can enslave. Designers incorporate "Sabbath reminders" into operating systems, nudging users to rest modes after cumulative screen hours. Testimonials from beta users report heightened creativity and deeper relationships once persuasive-design hooks are removed. These efforts echo Daniel's counter-diet proposal: he offered Babylon an alternative data diet to prove that covenant practices yield healthier outcomes. Success stories provide empirical leverage when lobbying governments for stronger data-protection laws, demonstrating that dignity-centric design is not only ethical but profitable.

9.3.4 Prophetic Disruption of Surveillance Cultures When ethical appeals fail, prophetic disruption steps in, mirroring Daniel's public prayer that defied the gag order. Activists release browser extensions that scramble ad-tracking pixels, turning data streams into digital glossolalia uninterpretable by marketing firms. Faith-based nonprofits publish transparency scorecards ranking tech companies on privacy, algorithmic bias, and employee well-being, influencing consumer choices. Pastors preach on Isaiah 47's downfall of Babylon, applying its exposure of hidden sorceries to modern predictive analytics that shape voters unknowingly. Intercessory teams prayer-walk around data centers, praying that any systems facilitating exploitation would malfunction until reformed. Lawyers file amicus briefs supporting whistle-blowers who reveal clandestine surveillance programs, citing Ephesians 5:11's call to expose the deeds of darkness. Journals run op-eds advocating "slow tech" legislation: mandatory "algorithmic sunsets" forcing periodic review of AI systems before renewal. Art collectives stage pop-up exhibits wherein participants walk through mazes of mirrored screens displaying their own metadata, driving home the visceral impact of constant observation. These varied acts form a tapestry of resistance, conveying that God sees every sparrow and thus His people need not bow to lesser watchers. The chapter moves from economic surveillance to economic integrity, maintaining the theme of holistic counter-formation.

9.4 Economic Pressures and Integrity

9.4.1 From Corruption to Consumer Debt Global supply chains can obscure injustices as effectively as Babylon's vast bureaucracy hid graft among satraps. Modern equivalents of royal kickbacks appear as bribes for contract bids, hidden environmental costs, and off-the-books labor. Developing-nation workers stitch fast-fashion garments for wages that barely cover housing, a reality remote shoppers seldom consider as they chase flash sales. Meanwhile, consumer debt climbs as credit cards entice buyers with "points" that disguise compounding interest. Proverbal wisdom warns that the borrower becomes slave to the lender (Proverbs 22:7); yet entire economies rely on revolving debt, normalizing servitude. Social-media influencers flaunt luxury hauls, pressuring followers toward unsustainable spending to keep pace with curated lifestyles. Beneath these pressures lurks a deeper issue: money isn't merely a medium of exchange but a rival deity promising security and significance. The Babylonian empire financed grand statues to reinforce glory; modern cultures erect megamalls and skyscrapers, architectural sermons extolling limitless consumption. Resisting corruption and debt starts with naming these forces as spiritual, not merely fiscal, threats, thereby reclaiming stewardship as an act of worship.

9.4.2 Stewardship Principles from Daniel's Portfolio Though best known for dreams and deliverance, Daniel managed royal assets, overseeing provincial revenues and resource allocation (Daniel 6:2-3). Scripture highlights his "exceptional spirit," which included transparent bookkeeping that thwarted satrap embezzlement.

Believers in finance sectors emulate this legacy by publishing third-party audit reports, voluntarily disclosing executive compensation, and refusing under-the-table commissions. Personal finance mirrors administrative stewardship: families construct zero-based budgets aligning every dollar with kingdom priorities, thereby converting earthly riches into friends for eternity (Luke 16:9). Churches teach envelope or digital-wallet systems where giving, saving, and spending categories reflect Proverbs' triad of generosity, foresight, and contentment. Young professionals adopt "graduated giving," increasing tithe percentages with each raise to counter lifestyle inflation. Marketplace entrepreneurs draft ethical supplier contracts that mandate living wages and environmentally responsible methods, forging micro-covenants reminiscent of Daniel's food test.

9.4.3 Jubilee Economics in Modern Markets Leviticus 25's jubilee legislation envisions systemic resets—land returned, slaves freed, debts canceled every fifty years. Contemporary adaptations include micro-loan forgiveness programs run by churches that purchase medical debt pennies on the dollar, liberating families from financial exile. Housing cooperatives employ shared-equity models giving renters ownership stakes without speculative risk, embodying Isaiah 58:6's call to "undo the straps of the yoke." Corporate tithe initiatives dedicate a fixed percentage of profits to community development, reframing success metrics beyond shareholder dividends. Faith-based venture funds seed minority-owned startups in underserved neighborhoods, demonstrating jubilee through economic inclusion. Municipal leaders influenced by Christian ethics propose property-tax holidays for elderly homeowners on fixed incomes, echoing sabbatical rest for land and labor alike. Each jubilee expression challenges scarcity mindsets, testifying that the earth and its fullness belong to the Lord (Psalm 24:1).

9.4.4 Vocational Discipleship for Financial Professionals Bankers, auditors, and investment managers occupy strategic gatekeeper roles akin to Daniel's satrap oversight. Vocational discipleship cohorts gather quarterly to examine real case studies—fraud detection, sustainable portfolios, whistle-blower dilemmas—and calibrate conscience through group discernment. Participants memorize verses addressing honest scales and free-from-love-of-money lifestyles (Leviticus 19:35-36; Hebrews 13:5), reciting them before client meetings as breath prayers. Mentors encourage junior analysts to set pre-decided ethical red lines—no participation in predatory lending, no structuring deals that hide risk in opaque derivatives. Professional guilds create "kingdom KPIs," measuring social impact alongside return on investment. When promotions hinge on compromising transparency, cohorts provide both moral support and networking leads to pivot careers if needed. This intentional formation equips financial insiders to embody Daniel's integrity, influencing economic systems for the common good. The transition from fiscal faithfulness to political peacemaking flows naturally, as money and power intertwine in public life.

9.5 Political Polarization and Kingdom Allegiance

9.5.1 Navigating Partisan Divides without Cynicism Modern democracies increasingly resemble echo chambers where algorithmic feeds reinforce tribal outrage. Friends unfollow relatives over election memes, and churches risk schism when sermons brush political themes. Cynicism tempts believers to disengage, muttering Ecclesiastes-like laments that "nothing new is under the sun." Yet Daniel, though captive under pagan kings, never withdrew from political engagement; he influenced policy while refusing idolatry. Wise navigation begins with media-diet audits—tracking daily screen time on partisan news and replacing surplus consumption with Scripture and longform journalism that presents multiple perspectives. Believers practice "political lectio," reading Isaiah 1's denunciation of unjust rulers and 1 Timothy 2's call to intercede for them, allowing revelation to calibrate emotional tone. Small groups stage listening circles where members explain why certain issues matter to them, cultivating empathy that defuses caricatures. These habits shift discourse from binary sloganeering to nuanced discernment rooted in love of neighbor.

9.5.2 Ambassadors of Reconciliation Paul writes that God entrusted us with the ministry of reconciliation (2 Corinthians 5:18–20), a calling that extends to civic fractures. Ambassadors host backyard dinners pairing ideological opposites under a covenant of civility—no interruptions, questions before rebuttals, prayers offered for shared concerns. Community theaters partner with churches to stage documentary plays weaving testimonies from all sides of contentious debates, transforming spectators into colamenters. Prayer-walks around legislative buildings ask God to soften hardened hearts and elevate common good over partisan gain. During election cycles, congregations fast from social media one day a week, meeting instead to intercede for honest campaigning. Believers trained in restorative-justice circles volunteer as mediators in neighborhood disputes, translating skills into political dialogue contexts. In workplaces, Christians defuse water-cooler rants by redirecting conversations toward shared aspirations for justice, security, and flourishing. Each peacemaking action embodies Jesus' beatitude that the peacemakers will be called children of God (Matthew 5:9).

9.5.3 Theology of Principled Pluralism Principled pluralism recognizes that, in a fallen yet restrained world, diverse convictions share civic space under God's common grace. Daniel's respect for pagan administrators—even as he rejected their idols—models this theology. Believers advocate for policies protecting dissenting voices, knowing that freedom secured for others safeguards the church when cultural winds shift. They resist majoritarian impulses within their own ranks, recalling Israel's exile as divine discipline for nationalistic presumption. Public theology courses teach Kuyper's sphere sovereignty and Augustine's City of God, helping leaders distinguish between penultimate political loyalties and ultimate kingdom allegiance. Town-hall forums facilitated by multi-faith panels demonstrate how principled pluralism fosters collaboration on homelessness or trafficking, while still preserving robust debate on doctrinal differences. Such frameworks inoculate disciples against culture-war rhetoric that portrays ideological opponents as existential threats rather than image-bearers.

9.5.4 Prophetic Patriotism Jeremiah urged exiles to seek Babylon's welfare even while denouncing its idols (Jeremiah 29:7). Prophetic patriotism similarly loves its homeland by praying, critiquing, and serving it, rather than abandoning or idolizing it. Churches celebrate national holidays by lamenting historical injustices and thanking God for common-grace gifts—justice systems, natural resources, linguistic heritage. Intercessors compose liturgical prayers naming government failures alongside courageous reforms, echoing Daniel's confession in chapter 9. Christian historians publish balanced textbooks that honor national achievements while exposing abuses, equipping students to love truth more than myth. Advocacy networks draft policy briefs shaped by biblical ethics—protecting the unborn, the immigrant, and the elderly—showing that kingdom allegiance enriches civic life. When patriotic symbols are co-opted for exclusionary agendas, believers gently but firmly reclaim them with inclusive narratives anchored in Genesis' declaration that all people arise from one blood. This prophetic patriotism positions the church as society's moral memory, similar to Daniel reminding Belshazzar of Nebuchadnezzar's humbling.

9.6 Crafting a Contemporary Rule of Resistance

9.6.1 Integrating Prayer Windows, Digital Boundaries, Financial Simplicity, and Civic Engagement

A contemporary rule of resistance weaves together visible prayer, intentional disconnection, lifestyle simplicity, and proactive public witness, forming a holistic framework for faithful dissent. Scheduling "prayer windows" at fixed daily intervals invites colleagues into respectful patterns of intercession, signaling that communion with God informs every professional decision (Daniel 6:10). In parallel, establishing digital boundaries—such as device-free mornings or evening tech curfews—creates spiritual breathing room, allowing the mind to attend to God rather than algorithms (Exodus 20:8). Financial simplicity counters consumerist pressure by capping discretionary spending, adopting transparent budgeting, and redirecting surpluses toward generosity, thus teaching the heart to trust God for provision (1 Timothy 6:17–19). Civic engagement anchors faith in public life, whether through voting informed by biblical justice principles, volunteering for restorative-justice initiatives, or testifying at city council meetings on behalf of marginalized neighbors (Micah 6:8). These disciplines reinforce one another: prayer windows empower civil action with divine wisdom; digital sabbaths free up time for community service; financial simplicity enables sustained generosity in advocacy work. Writing these commitments into a personal manifesto or "resistance rule" transforms good intentions into enforceable habits, reducing drift under pressure. Periodic reviews—quarterly or annual—assess fidelity to each element, prompting recalibration where habits have withered. Churches and small groups can offer workshops on drafting these blended rules, sharing templates and testimonies of efficacy. Over time, such integrated rules create countercultural islands of discipleship in secular seas, demonstrating that resistance requires both inward formation and outward action.

9.6.2 Community Covenants: Small-Group Charters for Mutual Accountability

No rule of resistance flourishes in isolation; covenantal bonds knit individuals into mutual pledges of fidelity. Small groups draft charters specifying shared commitments—praying together at set times, observing collective digital fasts, giving generously as a unit, and attending local civic forums on justice issues. These covenants outline practical details: meeting frequency, confidentiality agreements, and conflict-resolution processes, ensuring that accountability remains constructive rather than punitive (Galatians 6:1–2). By naming common threats—idolatrous work cultures, financial temptations, online echo chambers—the group defines its mission field and strategic focus, crafting targeted interventions such as joint letter-writing campaigns or corporate Sabbath proposals. Members rotate leadership roles to democratize responsibility and prevent burnout of key individuals. Digital platforms host covenant texts and progress reports, maintaining transparency while respecting privacy. When one member struggles—caught in a cycle of debt, embroiled in political discouragement, or slipping in prayer rhythms—the group mobilizes support: prayer bursts, financial coaching, or joint attendance at relevant advocacy events. Celebrating milestones—completing a month of Sabbath observance, volunteering at a justice center, or restoring a broken relationship—rewards perseverance and reinforces identity as a resistant community. These covenants echo early Jerusalem believers who held everything in common and devoted themselves to apostolic teaching and fellowship (Acts 2:42–47), demonstrating that collective fidelity multiplies individual resolve.

9.6.3 Measuring Faithfulness: Annual Examen of Habits, Relationships, and Public Witness

A rule of resistance requires regular health checks to avoid mechanical compliance or unexamined drift. An "annual examen" gathers the community to review each member's progress against the covenant charter, celebrating achievements and confessing lapse areas. For prayer rhythms, participants share insights gained and obstacles encountered; for digital boundaries, they discuss the impact on mental health and creativity; for financial simplicity, they report how generosity influenced personal contentment and community needs; for civic engagement, they assess the effectiveness of advocacy efforts and relationships formed in public spheres. This reflective season employs guiding questions: Which habits bore fruit? Where did we compromise? How have our identities as exiles shaped our vocational paths? Scripture passages such as Psalm 139:23–24 and Lamentations 3:40 frame the examen, inviting divine illumination of hidden blind spots. Each person writes personal goals for the coming year, anchored in kingdom priorities rather than cultural urgencies. The group commits to prayerful support for these objectives and schedules interim check-ins to foster momentum. By measuring faithfulness not by external applause but by covenantal alignment, communities maintain resilient hope, grounded not in results but in obedience (Hebrews 11:8–10). This disciplined self-assessment keeps the rule of resistance vital, dynamic, and responsive to new cultural challenges.

9.7 Bridge to the Epilogue—Heirs of an Unshakable Kingdom

9.7.1 Summarizing Daniel's Through-Line: From Exile Resilience to Apocalyptic Hope Tracing Daniel from deported youth to apocalyptic visionary reveals a unifying trajectory: faithfulness in small, unseen moments prepares the way for participation in God's grand redemptive narrative. His resistance in exile—refusing imperial food, interpreting foreign dreams, praying under threat—formed a character refined by conviction rather than comfort. Each trial deepened his reliance on the Ancient of Days, enabling him to receive revelations that spanned centuries. The apocalyptic visions that followed were not escapist fantasies but revelations for those already tested by lions and furnaces, equipping them to envision a world redeemed beyond the ruin of empires. This through-line teaches modern pilgrims that everyday disciplines—prayer windows, Sabbath rest, financial simplicity, prophetic engagement—are the launchpad for hope that outlasts systemic collapse. Summarizing this arc reminds readers that their present resistances, however small, invest them as heirs of the unshakable kingdom about to come.

9.7.2 Commissioning Readers as Modern "Wise Ones" Who Turn Many to Righteousness Belshazzar's empire fell because wise men failed to speak truth; Daniel's faithful counsel preserved a remnant. Now, readers are commissioned to become "wise ones" in their spheres—boardrooms, labs, courtrooms, classrooms—applying biblical insight to redirect the course of their communities. This calling echoes Daniel 12:3: "Those who are wise will shine like the brightness of the sky... and those who lead many to righteousness, like the stars forever." Practical equipping follows this commission: establishing mentorship networks, creating study cohorts, and mobilizing intercessory teams dedicated to cultural renewal. Churches host installation services where individuals affirm commitments to justice, truth, and compassion, laying hands as a symbolic passing of the prophetic mantle. Digital "star maps" document where participants serve—politics, art, business, education—encouraging cross-pollination of kingdom values across sectors. This commissioning ritual transitions the book's teaching into communal mission, forging a constellation of faithful witnesses in a world at risk of moral darkness.

9.7.3 Preview of Closing Benediction: Living, Leading, and Loving Against the World until the Son of Man Appears in Glory As the narrative arc closes, readers glimpse the final exhortation to embody Daniel's spirit of "walking against the world" with steadfast hope. The epilogue will unfold as a benediction that blesses those who refuse compromise, honors pathways of resistance shaped by Daniel's example, and imparts courage to continue loving enemies, seeking justice, and proclaiming mercy. It will call the faithful to live as ambassadors of the coming kingdom—leading in public institutions and loving their neighbors in the marketplace—until the ultimate appearance of the Son of Man transforms exile-lives into eternal fellowship. This preview invites anticipation: just as Daniel awaited the Ancient of Days, so we await the return of the heavenly King who writes our names in the Book of Life (Daniel 12:1; Revelation 20:12).

Conclusion

Walking against the world today demands more than sporadic acts of defiance; it calls for a sustained way of life shaped by disciplines that mirror Daniel's devotion and discernment. When faith intersects with contested spheres—minds shaped by relativism, bodies pressured by shifting norms, hearts targeted by algorithms, wallets strained by consumerism, and loyalties tested by partisanship—Christians can respond not with despair or withdrawal but with strategic engagement rooted in prayer, truth, and love. The practices outlined in this chapter—visible rhythms of intercession, communal accountability, Sabbath rest, economic simplicity, and peacemaking initiatives—form a cohesive rule of resistance that honors God and serves neighbor. As each believer embraces these habits, they contribute to a faithful remnant poised to steward God's justice in every corner of society, bearing witness to an unshakable kingdom that transcends the world's fleeting powers.

Chapter 10 – Living Daniel's Legacy: Forming Counter-Cultural Communities

In a world hungry for genuine connection and moral clarity, Daniel's story offers more than ancient intrigue—it provides a template for vibrant communities that embody the kingdom in the midst of exile. The prophet's life reminds us that faithful witness takes shape not only in solitary prayer but in the rhythms of shared devotion, mutual encouragement, and collective action. When small groups anchor their imaginations in Scripture, lament society's brokenness together, and extend hospitality as a countercultural sign of God's welcome, they create living laboratories of redemption. Daniel's mentorship of kings and his partnerships with peers demonstrate that influence flows most powerfully through relationships shaped by integrity and perseverance. As we explore practical practices—spiritual disciplines, intergenerational apprenticeship, public-square engagement, and covenantal rule-making—we discover how ordinary believers can cohere into prophetic households. These communities consecrate time, resources, and gifts not for comfort or status but for justice, peace, and hope. In doing so, they become the multiplied hope of a coming kingdom, ready to bless cities and reform institutions from within.

10.0 Why Communities Matter—From Lone Exiles to Prophetic Households

The book of Daniel opens with four teenagers torn from Jerusalem and concludes with a weathered prophet praying alone by the Tigris, yet every scene in between pulses with communal undercurrents that keep faith alive in a hostile world. Spiritual resilience is rarely a solo project; it takes shape in bands of friends who interpret dreams together, corporate fasts that recalibrate appetites, or all-night prayer vigils that hold fear at bay. Isolation, by contrast, leaves convictions exposed to the corrosive forces of flattery, compromise, and despair, much like embers that cool once removed from the hearth. Sociologists confirm what Scripture already assumes: practices multiply their formative power when enacted in groups, because habits reinforced by belonging sink deeper into the imagination and last longer under stress. A counter-cultural community therefore acts as a greenhouse for virtues that would otherwise wither in the draft of cultural hostility, providing relational scaffolding where courage can climb, confession can descend, and creativity can branch outward. When we speak of being "against the world," we do not mean withdrawal into monastic enclaves but rather an intentional stance that critiques idolatry while cultivating alternative economies of grace. Communities shaped by Daniel's legacy exhibit five distinctive marks. They are worshipful, centering identity on the holiness of God rather than on tribal affinities. They are hospitable, opening table and calendar to strangers so that solidarity replaces suspicion. They are discerning, testing cultural narratives against the canon of Scripture and the counsel of the Spirit. They are excellent, striving for skill that lends credibility to prophetic speech in boardrooms and classrooms alike. Finally, they are hopeful, rehearsing the coming kingdom until anticipation overwrites anxiety. These marks do not emerge accidentally; they require scaffolding—a rhythm of disciplines, mentoring pathways, public-square initiatives, and covenantal rules—that chapters 10.1 through 10.4 will construct brick by brick. As we move into the disciplines that undergird resilient witness, remember that every habit forged in personal devotion ripples outward, shaping households and congregations into prophetic households capable of blessing cities while resisting their idols.

10.1 Spiritual Disciplines for Resistance

10.1.1 Word-Anchored Imagination A community steeped in exile must learn to see reality through the lenses of revelation rather than the mirage of cultural slogans, and the primary tool for that recalibration is a sanctified imagination saturated in the Word. Lectio continua—systematic, slow-paced reading through entire biblical books—guards against proof-texting by embedding each verse in its covenant storyline. When groups gather to paint scenes from Jeremiah's potter or sing paraphrased psalms set to modern melodies, they engage multiple senses, allowing Scripture to sculpt neural pathways that advertisements cannot easily erode. Children who dramatize Daniel 3 discover kinesthetic memory of furnace fidelity, while adults who journal responses to Ezekiel's river vision cultivate an eschatological taste that no consumer brand can match. The goal is not information acquisition but narrative habitation: believers learn to inhabit the story in which beasts fall and saints inherit, thereby dethroning rival plots that promise salvation through status, romance, or technology. Weekly gatherings might devote fifteen minutes to a practice called "text and headline," where participants place a current news story beside a corresponding biblical passage—Amos beside wage-gap statistics, Revelation beside climate reports—allowing Scripture to critique and reframe public discourse. Over months, the imagination tutored by the Word begins to default to covenant reflexes: mercy over mockery, patience over panic, prophetic lament over cynical rant. Word-anchored imagination thus becomes the engine driving every other discipline, for fasting without Scripture devolves into wellness fad, lament without Scripture sinks into fatalism, and prayer without Scripture risks becoming a wish list unmoored from God's purposes.

10.1.2 Rhythms of Fasting and Lament Fasting is exile's protest against empires that feed bodies to numb souls, a declaration that man lives by every word from God's mouth (Matthew 4:4). Daniel's vegetable fast in chapter 1 was not a diet tip but a subversive refusal to baptize his identity in Babylonian luxury, and communities today echo that gesture when they abstain from algorithmic noise, sugar highs of instant shipping, or entertainment that commodifies intimacy. Quarterly "digital fasts" disconnect entire small groups from social platforms for seven days, opening relational bandwidth for neighborly presence and deep Scripture engagement. As hunger pangs or notification reflexes surface, members meet for communal lament liturgies that give language to grief over racial injustice, creation's groaning, or the global church's persecution. Lament is more than catharsis; it is covenant litigation, summoning God's promises into the courtroom of history much as Daniel pled for mercy in chapter 9. The liturgy may include antiphonal reading of Psalm 79, corporate silence punctuated by a single cello line, and responsive prayers that cycle through confession, accusation of evil, request for intervention, and recommitment to hope. These embodied practices train communities to metabolize sorrow without numbing, to channel anger toward redemptive petition rather than reactive outrage. Over time fasting and lament forge spiritual muscle memory: when crises erupt, the group instinctively gathers, abstains, prays, and waits rather than scapegoating or bingeing.

10.1.3 Convergent Prayer Practices Daniel's three-times-daily prayer was both a lifeline to heaven and a visible testimony to earth, and contemporary communities can replicate its power through layered patterns of solitary and collective intercession. Morning windows are personal: individuals set phone alarms that trigger brief kneeling rituals at bedside or commuter-train breath prayers invoking the day's Scripture focus. Midday convergence happens in micro-clusters—coworkers huddle in conference rooms for five silent minutes, students gather under a campus oak, construction crews form a prayer circle before lunch break—bearing witness that God's sovereignty permeates work hours. Evening watch returns families or roommates to a household altar, perhaps lighting a candle, singing a stanza of Psalm 134, and blessing local leaders by name. These converging streams create a current strong enough to carve prayer channels through institutional bedrock; HR departments eventually ask why employees pause together at noon, and neighborhood children learn that kitchens can function as sanctuaries. Integrating silence, sung psalms, and spontaneous petitions keeps the practice from calcifying into rote recital. Some groups adopt the "prayer-wheel" visual, dividing 60 minutes into twelve five-minute spoke segments—adoration, confession, scripture reading, petition, thanksgiving—to facilitate hour-long vigils before elections or budget approvals. The result is a community whose default reflex in crisis is to kneel, not to tweet, reflecting Paul's command to pray without ceasing (1 Thessalonians

5:17). These disciplines of Word, fast, lament, and prayer now flow naturally into pathways for transmitting wisdom across generations.

10.2 Mentorship and Inter-Generational Transmission

10.2.1 Daniel's Ripple Effect on Four Monarchs Daniel's influence spans some seventy years and at least four regimes, demonstrating that consistent character outlasts political turnover. His interpretation of Nebuchadnezzar's dream catalyzed a royal decree honoring Yahweh; his patient counsel guided Darius through administrative crisis; his prophetic letters likely informed Cyrus's liberation policy for exiles. Each episode shows mentorship operating vertically—prophet to king—contrary to modern assumptions that influence must come from formal authority. Today's believers translate this by cultivating relationships with supervisors, civic leaders, or school principals, offering thoughtful insight grounded in prayer rather than partisan talking points. They keep confident records, as Daniel kept visions sealed, ready to advise when trust capital opens a door. Such relational constancy teaches younger disciples that long obedience in the same workplace can yield kingdom leverage impossible to gain through platform chasing.

10.2.2 Apprenticing Youth for Babylon 2.0 Contemporary culture prepares adolescents for standardized tests and social branding but rarely for conscience collisions. "Lion's-Den labs" immerse teenagers in case studies: What if a history assignment requires affirming a view that contradicts biblical anthropology? How should a coding intern respond when asked to build persuasive micro-targeting software? Students role-play scenarios, then debrief using Daniel's framework: seek permission for alternate options, propose value-added solutions, accept consequences with grace. Layered mentoring pairs each teen with an older professional in the relevant field—science students with lab researchers, artists with studio mentors—so theoretical ethics meet vocational realities. Field trips to city councils or court hearings demystify public institutions, showing youth how prophetic presence can reform rather than merely critique. Over time, this pipeline produces graduates who enter universities fluent in both cultural exegesis and scriptural conviction, echoing Daniel 1:20's testimony of ten-fold superiority not only in knowledge but in wisdom.

10.2.3 Reverse Mentoring—Listening to Digital Natives Mentorship is a two-way street; elders bring theological depth while younger believers offer fresh discernment in tech-saturated contexts. Reverse-mentoring sessions invite high-school coders to teach retirees how apps harvest data, while retirees share contemplative practices that slow attention. Churches host inter-generational hackathons rewriting liturgies into immersive virtual-reality experiences, then evaluate theological fidelity together. This mutual submission models Ephesians 5:21, "submitting to one another out of reverence for Christ," dismantling age-based hierarchies that stifle innovation or wisdom. When older board members listen to Gen-Z on environmental stewardship, and Gen-Z listens to elders on sacrificial generosity, the body of Christ displays its manifold wisdom to principalities.

10.2.4 Covenant Story Nights Once a month, communities gather for a multigenerational storytelling evening. Seniors recount deliverances—escaping war zones, praying prodigals home, surviving medical crises—while children illustrate stories on butcher paper as they listen. Teenagers compose spoken-word responses, linking past miracles to present challenges like climate anxiety or mental-health struggles. The night closes with symbolic object exchange: an elder's worn Bible passed to a new believer, a teen's digital artwork gifted to the storyteller. Such rituals enact Psalm 78's mandate to tell God's deeds to the next generation, ensuring memory fuels mission. Audio recordings are archived in a "legacy library," accessible via podcast to diaspora members abroad, knitting scattered saints into one narrative fabric. These story nights do more than preserve history; they create expectancy that the God of Daniel still enters boardrooms, classrooms, and chatrooms today. As these intertwined disciplines and mentorship models take root, communities mature into prophetic households poised for missional presence outlined in section 10.3.

10.3 Missional Presence in the Public Square

10.3.1 Theology of Exile and Diaspora Engagement When Jeremiah wrote to the early exiles, he stunned them with a command to "seek the welfare of the city" that had just razed their temple (Jeremiah 29:7). Daniel's life supplies a living commentary on that verse, proving that exile is not a timeout from vocation but a redirected mission field. Theological reflection on diaspora begins by rejecting the twin errors of nostalgic withdrawal and triumphalist takeover; both stifle creative service and erode witness. Exile means accepting that earthly capitals will never mirror Zion perfectly while believing they can still experience foretastes of God's shalom. Practically, this posture re-labels ordinary civic arenas—parent-teacher meetings, neighborhood clean-ups, zoning hearings—as venues where covenant values can quietly rehumanize public life. Small groups read Esther alongside urban-planning articles, noticing how hidden influence can spare entire ethnic minorities. Seminary interns shadow city councillors to observe policymaking pressures, then pray on-site for wisdom and justice. Because exile is shared rather than solo, congregations map their members' geographic dispersions, identifying clusters able to collaborate on localized blessing projects. These efforts dismantle the false dichotomy between "church work" and "civic work," replacing it with the integrated vision Paul articulates when he calls believers "ambassadors" (2 Corinthians 5:20). As hearts absorb that identity, fear of cultural margins gives way to Spirit-empowered curiosity: What hidden gifts might God release through believers positioned in tech startups, social-services offices, or arts collectives? The theology of exile thus functions like a compass, orienting the rest of the community's public initiatives so they resist assimilation without lapsing into culture wars.

10.3.2 Embodied Advocacy for Justice Advocacy becomes truly Christian when it moves beyond hashtags into embodied proximity with the afflicted, echoing Christ's incarnational descent (Philippians 2:6-8). Daniel risked life to defend innocent wise men (Daniel 2:24); modern heirs emulate him when they stand in courtrooms as character witnesses for neighbors facing unjust eviction. Congregations form "court-watch teams" that sit silently during hearings, signalling public scrutiny that often reduces prosecutorial overreach. Others adopt a local foster-care agency, rotating Sabbath meals so case-workers taste hospitality rather than paperwork fatigue. Refugee legal clinics hosted in church basements pair pro-bono lawyers with translators from the congregation, offering holistic welcome that covers both legal status and relational belonging. Advocacy training includes Bible studies on Amos and modern documentaries about supply-chain exploitation, stirring lament that matures into strategic action. Participants draft letters to legislators but also ride buses to precinct meetings, because justice rarely emerges from distant commentary. Embodied service shapes moral imagination: once volunteers have washed the feet of street-corner sex workers, policy debates on human trafficking gain visceral urgency. These tactile ministries preach a sermon louder than slogans: God's kingdom restores dignity through sacrificial nearness, not remote condemnation.

10.3.3 Vocational Witness Networks Exile communities amplify impact when believers in similar sectors band together as guilds of excellence and integrity. Teachers gather monthly to workshop lesson plans that integrate literary classics with conversations about virtue, guarding against curricular drift that reduces education to test metrics. Healthcare professionals share anonymized case studies, discerning how to honour conscience in end-of-life scenarios without abandoning vulnerable patients. Software engineers form Slack channels where they peer-review one another's code for privacy protections before product launches, fulfilling Leviticus 19:14's call not to place a stumbling block before the blind. These networks function like Daniel's circle of friends: they pray, brainstorm creative alternatives to unethical mandates, and celebrate each member's public achievements as kingdom victories. Regular vocational retreats open with testimonies of God's faithfulness at work, followed by silent hikes that allow participants to process stress in creation's sanctuary. By the retreat's end, each professional leaves with a "mission experiment"—a defined action to infuse their workplace with covenant ethics over the next quarter. Such cross-pollination combats silo mentality and convinces isolated employees they are part of a wider resistance movement marked by competence and humility.

10.3.4 Hospitality as Prophetic Protest In a world where social bonds fray along political, racial, and economic lines, the dinner table becomes a radical stage for kingdom dramatization. Daniel's vegetable meal contested Babylonian assimilation; contemporary believers stage similar protests through inclusive feasts. Households adopt a "7-seat protocol," always leaving one chair open for strangers who might be international students, unhoused neighbors, or ideological opposites. Menus highlight locally sourced produce to honour creation care, reminding guests that stewardship begins with daily bread. Hosts listen more than lecture, modelling James 1:19's quick-to-hear posture that diffuses suspicion. Prayer before the meal intentionally names public anxieties—racial tension, market volatility—and invites God's peace into shared space. Stories flow over dessert, and by evening's end political caricatures soften into human faces bearing God's image. Some churches scale this practice city-wide, organising quarterly "common tables" that pair families from divergent zip codes, generating friendships that later birth collaborative justice projects. Hospitality also challenges consumerist rhythms by slowing time; multitasking phones rest face-down while candles burn low, signalling that people, not productivity, frame the evening's worth. Such prophetic banquets echo Jesus' table ministry, where tax collectors and zealots reclined side by side and discovered a new citizenship. The table thus becomes a micro-Eden where exile weariness gives way to anticipatory joy.

10.4 Crafting a Rule of Life

10.4.1 Personal Holiness Targets A rule of life translates abstract desire for holiness into concrete, measurable practices. Participants begin with a prayerful audit: reviewing calendars, bank statements, and screen-time reports to expose rival liturgies. From that data they craft specific targets—perhaps limiting social media to forty minutes daily, dedicating 10 percent of income to mercy initiatives, and reserving Monday evenings for silence and solitude. Targets also include verbal disciplines, such as committing to bless at least one coworker aloud each day, countering workplace cynicism with Proverbs 16:24 sweetness. Health habits matter too; Daniel's choice diet underscores a theology of the body, so members track sleep patterns and adopt moderate exercise as stewardship rather than vanity. Each target links to a Scripture promise, turning goals into covenant responses rather than self-help projects. Importantly, targets remain dynamic: quarterly reviews allow adjustments when seasons shift—new babies, job transitions, chronic illness.

10.4.2 Community Accountability Structures Once personal goals solidify, communal scaffolds ensure they stand amid cultural crosswinds. Triads meet in coffee shops for one hour: twenty minutes Scripture lectio, twenty sharing wins and failures, twenty interceding for next steps. Quads focus on mission execution, rotating leadership so every member learns facilitation. Mission cells adopt shared finances for specific projects, pooling micro-savings to fund refugee rent deposits or neighborhood art installations, turning abstract generosity into tangible impact. Groups sign confidentiality covenants to protect vulnerability, yet commit to Matthew 18 reconciliation when sin endangers the witness. A digital dashboard—accessible only to members—logs progress and prayer updates, fostering transparency without fostering legalism. Annual retreats include playful competitions—a reading challenge, screen-free streak, generosity milestone—because joy fuels endurance better than shame.

10.4.3 Liturgical Calendar Remix A counter-cultural community reshapes time, converting secular holidays from consumer frenzies into spiritual signposts. Epiphany is coupled with civil rights reflections, tracing light to Gentiles through stories of modern abolitionists. Lent overlaps tax season, prompting discussions on economic justice and charitable deductions. Pentecost inspires multilingual Scripture readings and immigrant testimonies, celebrating Spirit-empowered diversity against nationalistic narrowing. During Advent, families craft "waiting boxes" rather than wish lists, filling them with notes of unanswered prayers that will become Easter testimonies of provision or perseverance. Civic observances also receive theological reframes: Earth Day becomes a Sabbath earth-care festival where congregations plant trees and confess exploitation. By remixing calendars, believers inhabit an alternative storyline throughout the year, inoculating against marketing cycles that equate identity with consumption spikes.

10.4.4 Metrics and Milestones In business, key performance indicators guide strategy; communities of holiness deserve no less intentionality. Metrics track inputs—hours in Scripture, dollars given, volunteer shifts—and outputs—relationships reconciled, systemic changes influenced, baptisms celebrated. Story boards posted in fellowship halls visualize data: charts of reduced screen time, pies showing generosity allocation, maps plotting prayer-walk coverage. Each metric anchors a testimony night where numbers become narratives; for instance, a 30 percent decline in consumer debt translates into families funding micro-loan pools. Milestones are marked liturgically: completing a year of digital fasting rhythms culminates in an Ascension-day tech-on retreat to reflect on redeemed tools. Children receive "courage coins" when they practice classroom witness, linking small achievements with communal joy. Rather than fostering pride, metrics evoke gratitude that God empowers ordinary people to embody kingdom economics and habits within Babylon's gates.

10.5 Living in Maranatha Expectancy—Hope that Outlasts Empires

Hope is not mood optimism but disciplined imagination anchored in the certainty that Christ will return to judge and to renew. Daniel, even after receiving visions of beastly regimes, rose and "went about the king's business" (Daniel 8:27), proving that eschatological sight fuels vocational faithfulness rather than escapist withdrawal. Communities cultivate Maranatha expectancy by incorporating the Lord's return into daily doxology: morning greetings open with "The Lord is near" (Philippians 4:5), and bedtime prayers surrender unresolved anxieties to the coming Judge. Artists paint murals of Isaiah's wolf-and-lamb peace on church walls, reminding children that violence has an expiry date. Economists craft budgets assuming Christ may tarry decades yet could appear tomorrow, balancing long-term investment with present-day generosity. Funeral liturgies culminate not in finality but in the acclamation "Come, Lord Jesus," projecting grief into resurrection hope. Weekly communion rehearses wedding-banquet anticipation, nourishing perseverance more effectively than motivational slogans. Families mark suffering anniversaries—loss of a job, diagnosis day—with small feasts celebrating God's sustaining presence and previewing the greater feast to come, echoing Paul's claim that present sorrows are "light and momentary" compared with eternal weight (2 Corinthians 4:17). Mission teams enter unreached zones believing their labour hastens the day when every tribe will join heaven's chorus (Matthew 24:14), thus reframing risk as investment in inevitability. Maranatha expectancy also tempers political engagement: citizens advocate boldly yet refuse apocalyptic despair when policies fail, because ultimate governance rests on the shoulders of the Prince of Peace (Isaiah 9:6). Finally, this hope dignifies aging saints; retirement parties bless elders as "future immortals" whose wisdom will shine like stars forever (Daniel 12:3). Through such rhythms, communities live with feet firmly planted in contested streets and eyes fixed on the horizon where the Son of Man approaches in glory, ready to end exile once and for all.

10.5 Living in Maranatha Expectancy—Hope that Outlasts Empires

Hope shaped by the certainty of Christ's return transforms everyday routines into anticipatory rehearsals of the age to come. When communities greet one another with "Maranatha—Come, Lord"— they declare that history's final chapter belongs not to political powers but to the Son of Man (1 Corinthians 16:22). This hopeful salutation becomes a spiritual warp and weft in which present suffering is woven into eternal triumph. Houses of worship display banners quoting Revelation's invitation, reminding congregants that their prayers and praise contribute to a cosmic liturgy yet to reach crescendo. Neighborhood groups plant "resurrection gardens," small plots where seeds are sown with the prayer that life will emerge from apparent death, symbolizing both spring's renewal and the firstfruits of the resurrection (1 Corinthians 15:20). Families mark "anticipation Sundays" quarterly, inviting children to craft "welcome home" cards for the returning King, reinforcing that waiting is itself a form of worship. Even corporate boardrooms begin meetings with a brief meditation on Daniel's legacy of faith under pressure, reframing profit-and-loss statements within the context of ultimate deliverance. Pastors preach eschatological sermons that balance warnings of judgment with promises of restoration, avoiding either grim fatalism or superficial optimism. Care teams accompany the grieving through loss by reading Daniel 12:2 aloud, affirming that death's finality is a false witness to heaven's certainty. Worship playlists include both laments and triumphal anthems, reflecting the "already/not yet" tension of our pilgrim status. Church newsletters feature testimonies of small mercies—healed relationships, unexpected provision—portrayed as foretastes of the coming fullness. Missionaries return to share how distant villages sing new songs about a kingdom that local despotism cannot extinguish. Even liturgical colors carry eschatological meaning: violet encourages penitence in Advent, gold adorns spaces during Epiphany, and white bursts forth at Easter dawn celebrations. Youth groups compose futuristic psalms, setting biblical lyrics to electronic beats to connect with tech-savvy teens. Bible colleges offer courses on "Kingdom Creativity," teaching students to design art installations, theater pieces, and digital experiences that evoke eschatological hope. Senior adult ministries host prayer breakfasts where elders recount lives spanning multiple decades of change, testifying that no earthly upheaval has unraveled God's purposes. These interlocking practices cultivate emotional resilience, because when disappointments and injustices abound, the soul anchored in Maranatha expectancy neither collapses under despair nor drifts into apathy. Instead, it stands firm, fueled by the promise that Jesus will return on clouds of glory (Daniel 7:13–14), establishing an unshakable kingdom that outlasts every empire.

10.6 Bridge to the Closing Benediction—From Ancient Courts to Modern Cities

10.6.1 Summarizing Daniel's Through-Line: From Exile Resilience to Apocalyptic Hope

Daniel's story unfolds as a tapestry woven with threads of unwavering devotion, courageous dissent, prophetic revelation, and steadfast hope. From his first act of dietary resistance to his final vision of cosmic renewal, his life models how private disciplines seed public transformation. Early chapters show that small-scale fidelity—choosing vegetables over royal delicacies, kneeling in prayer despite decrees—accumulates moral capital that sustains larger interventions. Mid-book narratives demonstrate how covenant loyalty under exile yields imperial decrees protecting conscience, illustrating that personal witness can reshape state policy. His apocalyptic visions, received after seasons of trial, cast these episodes into a grand narrative that connects earthly trials with heavenly purposes. This through-line teaches that each discipline, whether personal or communal, connects sequentially: prayer fuels courage; integrity invites revelation; revelation ignites hope; hope energizes action. Modern believers, too, trace this trajectory by integrating inner formation with outward witness, ensuring that activism springs from contemplative roots. Churches recast their annual calendars to mirror Daniel's progression—fasting seasons precede preaching on deliverance, which in turn sets the stage for teaching on apocalyptic hope. Staff retreats involve workshops that map organizational goals onto Daniel's five-stage pattern: conviction, courage, counsel, cosmic vision, and kingdom living. This summary invites readers to recognize where they stand on the arc and to anticipate the final steps: commissioning as "stars" to guide others into righteousness (Daniel 12:3).

10.6.2 Commissioning Readers as Modern "Wise Ones" Who Turn Many to Righteousness

Just as Daniel stood before kings as God's messenger, today's disciples are commissioned to carry covenant wisdom into every sphere of influence. Commissioning ceremonies take place during worship services or small-group gatherings, where leaders lay hands on those entering new vocations—teachers, nurses, programmers, artists—praying that their expertise would become channels of divine insight. Participants receive a "Daniel's Mandate" booklet outlining practical steps for moral courage in fields vulnerable to compromise, such as finance, law enforcement, and entertainment. Mentors present graduates with symbolic gifts—scroll replicas, engraved compasses, or custom-made pens symbolizing prophetic writing—embedding the commission in tangible tokens. Each recipient declares a vow drawn from Daniel 1:8–9: to resolve in heart not to defile themselves and to ask for wisdom from above. Commissioned groups form "Constellation Networks," interlinked cohorts across professions that meet virtually to share breakthroughs and strategize interventions. Press releases accompany major commissioning events, signaling to broader communities that a new cohort of "wise ones" now walks among them. These rituals shift the identity of participants from passive believers to proactive ambassadors, echoing 2 Corinthians 5:20's call to reconciliation ministry. Those commissioned return to their schools, offices, and neighborhoods carrying the authority of a gathered church behind them, ready to bring many to righteousness through exemplary character and articulate testimony.

10.6.3 Preview of Closing Benediction: Living, Leading, and Loving Against the World until the Son of Man Appears in Glory

As the book draws to a close, readers are invited to prepare their hearts for a final blessing that both summons and sustains. The closing benediction will echo Daniel's climactic imagery of stars and crowns, commissioning each participant to shine in darkened arenas until the dawn of Christ's advent. It will offer scriptural benedictions—Numbers 6:24–26's Lord's face shining, Revelation 22:20's "Yes, come Lord Jesus"—weaving together prayer and prophetic assurance. Practical application follows: every household will be encouraged to hang a "Maranatha plaque" by their main entrance, symbolizing ongoing expectancy. Offices will receive digital wallpapers featuring the Ancient of Days and seven-star emblems, visually reminding employees of cosmic oversight. School groups will craft classroom posters quoting Daniel's promise that those who teach righteousness shine forever (Daniel 12:3). Neighborhood ministries will distribute maranatha prayer cards at community events, inviting every resident to join the anticipation. The benediction will thus transform from page into pulpit into pavement, sending God's people forth with both the authority of the living God and the humility of exiles trusting His timing. As it is pronounced, congregations will stand, raise hands, and release one another with words forged in the fires of exilic devotion, marking a rite of passage from study into missional enactment. The final blessing will carry both comfort for those weeping under oppression and challenge to those wielding influence, reminding all that the world's powers are temporary and heaven's kingdom eternal. And so, with voices joined in "Maranatha," the church steps into every sector of society, ready to live Daniel's legacy until the Son of Man appears in glory.

Conclusion

Forming countercultural communities is not an optional addendum to personal piety but the very soil in which resilient faith takes root. Daniel's legacy challenges us to move beyond sporadic acts of defiance and toward sustained patterns of live-in solidarity that nourish both individual virtue and societal transformation. When believers commit to shared disciplines, mentor across generations, and engage the public square with embodied compassion, they weave a network of witnesses that no empire can fully suppress. Crafting a rule of life—blending prayer, Sabbath, simplicity, and service—anchors these communities amid shifting cultural currents. Together, they practice Maranatha expectancy, living each day in the light of the Son of Man's promised return. In this way, Daniel's ancient example becomes our contemporary commission: to stand firm in exile, to build prophetic households, and to anticipate the unshakable kingdom that will never end.

www.ingramcontent.com/pod-product-compliance
Lightning Source LLC
Chambersburg PA
CBHW060319050426
42449CB00011B/2551